Praise for *Let There d.light*

"A unique book about a unique company that is changing the world. Let there be d.light."

SETH GODIN, AUTHOR OF *THIS IS MARKETING*

"The road from an idea to a successful business is only straight and smooth in the rearview mirror. To travel it in emerging markets is even harder. *Let There d.light* chronicles such an adventure but with a major difference: the final destination, instead of riches, is to impact the vulnerable lives of the majority of humanity. That makes it a story that truly matters."

MICHAEL CHU, HARVARD BUSINESS SCHOOL, AND CO-FOUNDER, IGNIA PARTNERS LLC

"The d.light story provides a window into the distinctive group of visionary entrepreneurs who have powered the creation of a vibrant off-grid solar industry. The social enterprise model of d.light has become a beacon for a new generation of entrepreneurs looking to attack an array of previously intractable development issues across the world. A great read, this is the adventure of a couple of special young guys whose experience as entrepreneurs provides hope for a better world."

RUSSELL STURM, GLOBAL LEAD FOR ENERGY ACCESS, INTERNATIONAL FINANCE CORPORATION

"If you are intrigued by the potential of for-profit social entrepreneurship and you enjoy a roller-coaster ride, read this book! The d.light story illustrates what is possible when a small, young team, imbued with unending perseverance and resourcefulness, tackles the seemingly impossible goal of enabling one hundred million customers in developing economies to transition from kerosene fuel to solar power. The d.light founders, together with the organization and products they have built, are exemplars of the very best that the Stanford Design for Extreme Affordability Program has produced."

JAMES PATELL, HERBERT HOOVER PROFESSOR OF PUBLIC AND PRIVATE MANAGEMENT, EMERITUS, & CO-FOUNDER OF THE DESIGN FOR EXTREME AFFORDABILITY PROGRAM, STANFORD UNIVERSITY

"*Let There d.light* is a great book about the journey of exceptional people building an exemplary and impactful social business—with a bit of luck, but mostly with massive passion, perseverance and sweat. Anyone seeking to grow their own social business, and anyone seeking to invest in one, should learn a lot from their story. After reading this, no one should ever think this is easy."

KOEN PETERS, EXECUTIVE DIRECTOR, GOGLA

LET THERE d.light

How one social enterprise brought solar products to 100 million people

DORCAS CHENG-TOZUN

Palo Alto | Nairobi | Gurgaon | Shenzhen

Cover design by Dorcas Cheng-Tozun
Cover copyright © d.light, Inc.
Images courtesy of d.light, Dorcas Cheng-Tozun, Angela Cheung, Erica Estrada, Robin Chilton, Ti El Attar, Sam Goldman, Karl Skare, Theo Steemers, Ned Tozun, and Xianyi Wu

First edition: July 2020

The d.light name and logo are trademarks of d.light, Inc.

d.light USA
2100 Geng Road, Suite 210
Palo Alto, CA 94303
dlight.com
facebook.com/dlightdesigninc
twitter.com/dlightdesign
instagram.com/dlightdesigninc

ISBN: 978-1-7343970-0-0 (paperback)

*To d.light customers around the world,
who have generously shared their lives with us
and welcomed us into their homes*

Contents

Foreword

BY JACQUELINE NOVOGRATZ, CEO, ACUMEN

One of my greatest joys as the CEO of Acumen, a global organization focused on investing the right kind of capital in the right kind of character to create change for the poor, is spending time with our companies' customers. In March 2016, in a far-flung village in Rajasthan, India, I noticed d.light lanterns hanging from the roofs of nearly every household. Sitting with a group of low-income, mostly illiterate women, I asked why they had switched from kerosene, a fuel they had used for generations despite its being dirty and expensive, to a d.light solar product.

The women offered an array of responses:

"The solar doesn't make my house dirty or my children sick."

"I can carry the lamp to the toilet at night and no longer have to fear the snakes in the area."

"When my children are frightened in the night, I can turn on the light and soothe them."

Having been invested in d.light for nearly a decade by then, I had heard such responses often. Women and men alike are ecstatic once they make the transition to solar. For the first time in their lives, they can illuminate the darkness with a flick of a switch. And no matter how poor, most low-income households can afford a US$4 d.light lantern.

Then, a slender woman dressed in fuchsia and violet leaned forward, holding her bright orange d.light lantern as she peered into my eyes. "Madam, when I had depended on kerosene, I was always feeling stressed that the lantern might fall over and burn my children. Now I feel satisfied that they will be safe. That is my reason for switching."

Now it was my turn to stare. "Madam," I said, "the young man who started this company was living in a West African village when his neighbor's son was badly burned in a kerosene accident. That was the moment that Sam Goldman made a resolution to find a way to eradicate kerosene. Soon after, he and his partner Ned Tozun came together to build the company that produced the solar lantern you purchased to keep your family safe."

The woman's eyes welled up as she continued to hold my gaze. "Please, Madam, thank those young men for me."

Imagine being thanked by someone on the other side of the world for your efforts. Imagine *one hundred million people* who are living better lives because of your boldness, your persistence. That is the story of d.light, a story of dreaming big and starting small; of imagining a better world where people don't have to live in darkness just because they are poor, and then building it; a story of listening, of patient urgency, of never, ever giving up.

Ultimately, d.light is the story of success redefined. Sam, Ned, and the remarkable d.light team have been motivated not by money, power, or fame, but by a commitment to solve one of global poverty's toughest problems: the lack of electricity. In 2006, the co-founders created a purpose-driven company. They listened first and foremost to those they intended to serve, learned to partner with a wide range of stakeholders, and never lost sight of their North Star. Fourteen years later, the company stands as a successful, scaled business model for an inclusive, sustainable company in an age of raging inequality and a climate emergency. Even more, the company helped spark a revolution in off-grid solar energy, a sector with the potential to solve the problem of energy poverty while also helping to avert a long-term climate crisis.

For more than a decade, d.light has been one of Acumen's greatest partners and most effective teachers. The company taught us what it means to use the market as a listening device, relying on human-centered design to create the right products for people who have been invisible for too long. d.light helped us understand that it was not enough simply to "build a better mousetrap" for the poor. The company had to overcome issues of low income, low trust, and poor infrastructure while confronting an abundance of bureaucracy, corruption, and complacency.

d.light also contended with significant external events. Without a large financial cushion, the company's team had to rely on their own persistence to build products and services that met their customers' needs at prices they could afford. That is a tall order, yet that is the work of disruptive change. It requires the audacity to remain focused on the horizon and the humility to confront the realities of the world around you.

When I speak of d.light now, listeners conclude that this company would be a no-brainer for an investor. This was not the case in its early years, when the business struggled mightily, needing to learn to price and market a product specifically aimed at the poor, and to partner with corporations, nonprofit organizations, and governments. Grit and resilience, bolstered by partnership and hope, played no small role in the company's success.

d.light has taught Acumen the importance of investing *more than* capital in companies serving the poor. Over a ten-year period, more than ten individual Fellows (our program to identify, develop, link, and celebrate entrepreneurial leaders with the moral imagination to effect change) spent nearly a year each with d.light, contributing to the company's overall operations. In turn, these individuals, like so many team members at d.light, caught the social impact "bug," founding or helping to build important social enterprises, many in the off-grid energy sector.

To calculate d.light's overall impact is to count not only the 100 million lives that are lighter, brighter, and more secure, but to calculate the thousands of jobs created for young people across the world who can now contribute to building their nations and regions. In this, the d.light team has not only built a company. It has built nations.

I think of Mary, a Kenyan agent who lived in a two-room house in a rural area outside of Taita, about an hour's drive from Nairobi. Though Mary earned very little income, she initially refused to accept payment from d.light despite being one of their most effective salespeople in Nairobi.

"I am not an agent," she told me, smiling confidently. "Me, I am an angel. You see, I am sixty-eight years old. Before I die, I want to know that I have done something meaningful to give back to my country. What better thing can I do but encourage my neighbors and their neighbors to invest in their own lives and improve our community?"

It has been one of Acumen's greatest adventures to partner with d.light. The company has helped Acumen become a better investor. We have learned that with the right kind of capital invested in the right character—entrepreneurs who operate from a place of moral leadership, putting the poor first and building a company from a place of purpose *before* profits—we can make the impossible possible.

d.light's story stands as a primer for anyone interested in the hard, sometimes thankless, but ultimately deeply meaningful and productive work of social change. And Ned Tozun and Sam Goldman will stand forever as two of the most successful role models I have ever met.

Here's to the next decade of illuminating the lives of millions more.

Chapter 1

SAM GOLDMAN

Almost nothing about Sam Goldman's childhood was conventional. His parents worked for the United States Agency for International Development (USAID). His father was an agricultural economist who became a USAID mission director, while his mother was a disaster relief officer and a specialist in public health and nutrition.

Sam was born in the U.S. but went to Cameroon when he was only fourteen days old, spending his infancy and toddlerhood accompanying his mother on long, dusty Land Rover rides to remote villages in the arid north and forested western regions. Every few years after that, the family would receive a new assignment to another country and relocate together.

As a result, Sam lived in Mauritania while in preschool, in Pakistan during elementary school, in Peru for middle school, and in India during high school. Throughout this time, Sam attended international schools brimming with students from dozens of countries around the world. He also occasionally accompanied his parents in their field work.

"I had the best of both worlds," Sam explains. "We had a lot of amenities that people in government and business had, but I also got to see what life was really like in emerging and underdeveloped economies. My childhood was full of love and adventure and diversity."

His parents' work came with its fair share of risks. Sam remembers how an ammunitions dump in Islamabad, Pakistan, once caught on fire. Bombs and missiles landed all over the city— including on the campus of his school, forcing all the students to hide in the gymnasium.

When the family was in Peru, the country was in the middle of two decades of severe instability while government forces and insurgent groups battled for control.[1] Sam recalls how bombings— which often targeted American businesses or institutions—were a regular occurrence.

Once, just as his family was pulling out of the airport after picking up Sam's grandparents, a portion of the airport exploded.

"Was that a bomb?" Sam's grandfather asked.

"Oh, it could be anything," his father replied smoothly. "It's getting late," he added as he ushered them into a bulletproof vehicle for the ride home.

By the time Sam went to college, he wanted a liberal arts education and a more conventional existence close to the Canadian side of his family. He chose to attend the University of Victoria in British Columbia, Canada, majoring in biology and minoring in environmental studies. "I loved plants and life," he says. "I mostly wanted to protect it." While in Victoria, he spent as much time as he could outdoors, hiking and camping through pristine Canadian wilderness on Vancouver Island.

But the developing world continued to pull on him. In between his years in university, Sam engaged in various internships around the world to learn and gain valuable experience. He spent one summer working with his parents on development projects in India; he spent another summer supporting conservation efforts to protect the golden monkey in Rwanda.

Sam finished his undergraduate studies with the certainty that he wanted to do something with a meaningful social and environmental impact. He also realized that, even after all his experience in different countries, he did not actually know what the day-to-day experience of a subsistence farmer was. This led him to apply to the Peace Corps, a US government-run volunteer program that promotes social and economic development in other countries.

Sam heard that his application was accepted as he was bicycling across Canada with thirty other members of the Climate Change Caravan to educate Canadians on reducing their carbon footprint. The Peace Corps asked if he would consider going to Mauritania for two years. Sam did some research and, deciding he didn't want to battle the Sahara Desert, asked for a different assignment. The Peace Corps offered to send him to Benin, a tiny nation in West Africa with about seven million people.

As Sam learned about Benin through Internet cafés along his bike route, he became increasingly fascinated with its rich history and wide array of ethnic groups and languages. A fellow biker named Tim had spent time in Benin and really loved it. He, along with other family friends, made the case that Sam could make a significant impact in such a small, resource-poor country. And because Benin is relatively stable, Sam's efforts wouldn't be destroyed by war or conflict—something his parents had experienced before. "If Benin is good enough for Tim, then it's good enough for me," Sam remembers thinking.

After Sam completed three months of mandatory training, he was sent to a village in the middle of Benin called Guinagourou. The village had about one to two thousand residents, all of whom lived without electricity, running water, or mobile connectivity. Nearly all

Sam in Benin with his main mode of transport

the residents were subsistence farmers who struggled to provide for their large families. But there were also positive signs of growth in the village: they had a primary school, a new health center, and plans for an additional primary school and secondary school.

In early 2002, Sam arrived at the three-room mud house that would be his home for the next three years. He recalls how the house was full of crumbling mud and the door was hanging off its hinges. There was also no bathroom or shower. In addition to beginning his work as an environmental action volunteer, Sam spent more than six months working to improve his residence. He added cement to the walls. He built his own pit latrine, shower, fence, and chicken coop. He worked with local masons and welders to build secure doors and furniture.

In the meantime, Sam was partnering with villagers and local masons to create extremely low-cost rain catchment systems to help tide families over during the long dry season, and to build pit latrines to improve sanitation in Guinagourou and nearby villages. He restarted an abandoned agricultural training center to instruct unemployed youth on animal husbandry and growing improved crop varieties.

Eventually, he learned about a plant called moringa, which is often called "the miracle plant." He started a non-governmental organization (NGO) with a local friend that taught women how to grow moringa, turn it into a powder, and sell it to local health centers as nutritional supplements for pregnant women and malnourished children.

Events were conspiring, though, to awaken Sam to the importance of light in off-grid regions. There are three incidents that remain seared in his memory.

A few months after arriving in Guinagourou, Sam had become accustomed to using a kerosene lantern for light at night, just as his neighbors did. One night, as he walked into his kitchen to get more food for a visiting friend, he felt a sharp pain in his toe. He dropped his lantern in surprise; the flame immediately went out. Sam knew that he had been bitten by a snake. Unfortunately, in the total darkness, he couldn't see what kind of snake it had been.

His neighbors worried that Sam had been bitten by a highly venomous green mamba, which can kill its victims in only thirty minutes. It wasn't until the next morning that the snake was found.

Sam with the students in the environmental club in Guinagourou

It turned out to be a relatively harmless green tree snake. But that was only after a frantic night in which Sam had to borrow money to pay for a motorcycle ride to a health center seven kilometers away, where he was given their last dose of antivenom, hoping against hope that he wasn't going to die.

A few months later, Sam was attending a death ceremony in the village, full of drumming and dancing, when the rented generators stopped working. Everything stopped as the event was thrown into complete darkness.

Sam had recently purchased a secondhand US$10 LED headlamp from another American volunteer. He turned on that headlamp and held it up as high as he could. In the pitch black, that single lamp provided enough light for the hundreds of attendees. The drumming and dancing promptly began again amidst loud cheering and rising dust clouds.

Then came the kerosene accident. One day in 2004, Sam had ridden his bike to the nearest town, forty-five kilometers away, to purchase some groceries and basic supplies. When he returned, he heard the news: his neighbor's fourteen-year-old son, who had participated in Sam's primary school environmental club, had tried to refuel a kerosene fridge. As is common for kerosene purchased on the black market, the fuel had been adulterated. When the boy tried to light the oil, it had exploded. He had been badly burned over most of his body.

Sam remembers stepping into his neighbor's courtyard and seeing the boy lying facedown on the ground. His back was coated in leaves and herbal pastes to treat his burns. It would take him years and multiple operations to recover. The scars, of course, would always be there.

That was when Sam began to research the dangers of kerosene. There were thousands of cases of fires caused by kerosene lanterns each year, leading to lost property, severe burns, and thousands of fatalities. Fumes from burning kerosene also cause upper respiratory conditions and other health issues.[2] And, as Sam knew from personal experience, kerosene lanterns are a terrible—and terribly expensive—source of light.

As he thought about the technology available in the twenty-first century, Sam became increasingly frustrated that 1.6 billion people, or nearly one quarter of the world's population, still had to rely on kerosene for light. And no one was filling this need. Sam began writing to LED lantern companies, explaining the huge market opportunity in West Africa and his interest in being a distributor. Not a single one responded.

Sam with his neighbors, including their son who was injured in the kerosene accident (third from left)

So, in his third year in the Peace Corps, Sam took a sharp turn in his career. His commercial work with his moringa NGO had shown him that business could be a powerful force for social change. But he needed to learn more about establishing and scaling a business. He decided to apply for business school.

That wasn't easy to do from a village in Benin. Sam had to bike forty-five kilometers just to access the internet to research schools. He also had to travel all the way to Accra, Ghana, to take the GMAT, the business school entrance exam. It took him an entire month to cross two countries to get there, as the secondhand motorcycle he bought for the trip kept breaking down.

While doing research online, Sam found a 2001 report called "Beyond Grey Pinstripes," published by the World Resources Institute and The Aspen Institute.[4] The report listed the leading business schools for social impact management and environmental management. He applied to the top five MBA programs, including the Stanford Graduate School of Business (GSB). In particular, Stanford's business school was collaborating with the newly formed Hasso Plattner Institute of Design in a class called Entrepreneurial Design for Extreme Affordability that caught Sam's eye.

A few months later, while traveling in Ghana after the completion of his Peace Corps assignment, Sam was in a drum class when his drum teacher got a call. It was the dean of admissions of the Stanford business school, calling to congratulate Sam for being accepted. "I think I treated myself to a can of Pringles that night," he says, laughing. "I had absolutely no idea how competitive Stanford was until I got there."

Even then, Sam wasn't sure he wanted to attend Stanford. He had received acceptances from other schools, including a couple with generous scholarship packages. But his parents strongly encouraged him to go to Stanford, and he eventually agreed.

For the first time, Sam moved to the United States to live long term. After saving every penny he could on a daily stipend of US$5 a day while in the Peace Corps, he was shocked by the affluence of the San Francisco Bay Area. But his experience at Stanford was everything he had hoped for and more. "Everyone was amazing. It was very exhilarating," he recalls.

And the highlight, by far, was the Entrepreneurial Design for Extreme Affordability class that he enrolled in during his first semester. "In terms of changing the wiring of my brain, that class has altered it more than many things in my life," Sam says. "It appealed to the creative process. It pushed barriers. It encouraged me to challenge myself."

It was also the perfect vehicle to help launch Sam's dream of building a business with the potential for huge social impact.

Myanmar: The First d.light Customer

Mi-Ya, a single mother of five children, was accustomed to staying up all night, making bricks and laying them out so they could begin drying as soon as the sun rose. She worked by the light of a candle because kerosene and diesel were too expensive for her.

Sam Goldman and Ned Tozun met Mi-Ya on their first trip to Myanmar in December 2006. She was given one of their earliest prototypes: a few LEDs connected to a sealed-lead-acid battery.

A few days later, Sam and Ned returned to find that Mi-Ya had gathered together cash in hopes of purchasing the prototype. With tears in her eyes, she said her entire family's lives had changed. Her kids were no longer coughing or experiencing eye irritation; she was able to work more efficiently; there even seemed to be fewer mosquitoes around them.

Her enthusiasm for the light convinced Sam and Ned that they had to make d.light into a real company that could provide such life-changing solutions.

"I still think of Mi-Ya as the first d.light customer," Ned says.

Chapter 2

NED TOZUN

Growing up in the Silicon Valley, Ned Tozun had a pretty different childhood from Sam's. Outside of school hours, he liked playing video games, riding his bike around the region's many trails, and learning to code from his engineering father. As a teenager, he became particularly interested in music, and spent hours playing the guitar and composing original songs.

But one thing that Ned had in common with Sam was a connection to the world outside the U.S. His father had immigrated to the U.S. from the unrecognized country of the Turkish Republic of Northern Cyprus, and Ned spent quite a few summers visiting relatives there.[5] It was a world away from Silicon Valley.

"Because of its unrecognized status, Northern Cyprus didn't have access to most of the things that were common in the U.S.," Ned remembers. "There was no air conditioning, even in one-hundred-degree weather. The power would go out a lot." Those long trips instilled in him an understanding that life looked very different in other parts of the globe. There were many communities that didn't have access to the technologies and opportunities that were commonplace in California. Modern conveniences, he realized, might be the exception rather than the norm.

Ned's idyllic childhood came to an abrupt and painful end during his second year as an undergraduate student at Stanford University, when his father passed away unexpectedly. As an only child, he was extremely close to both his parents.

Losing his father forever altered Ned's sense of who he was. His dad had had near-celebrity status in his Turkish Cypriot community as a successful athlete, musician, and student who had won a prestigious scholarship to study in the United States. More than two decades after leaving his home country, he was still beloved by many there.

Ned as a teenager with his father on a family trip to Northern Cyprus

Ned felt a sudden responsibility to live up to what his father had achieved. "I felt like I had to do something big to fill his shoes, but I had no idea what that would be," he remembers. Even as he grieved, he pushed himself to find the area of study that would enable him to accomplish the most. He dabbled in music, then engineering. He also considered physics, biology, and environmental sciences. At the start of nearly every quarter, Ned changed his major and enrolled in an entirely different set of classes.

Over time, he found the idea of specializing to be increasingly unappealing. Everything fascinated him; he wanted to learn as much as he could about as many things as possible. Out of necessity, he finally settled on computer science and earth systems degrees. But even then, he wasn't sure what career he wanted to pursue.

In his first job after college, Ned worked as an engineer, developing sound-mixing consoles for film studios. It was a great job on the surface, but a poor fit for Ned. "It was a soul-sucking experience," he remembers. Six months later, he quit.

Ned started his first company with a couple of friends. Together, they composed and produced personalized music albums. This was Ned's earliest experience with the hard work of business development and sales. He and his business partners searched for musical collaborators and distributors; they pitched their products to online retailers and brick-and-mortar stores. They experienced some success, but there were far more disappointments along the way.

Despite this, Ned found the work exhilarating. He realized that he loved building a business from scratch. He loved applying creativity and hard work to solving challenging business problems. "I am very similar to my dad in this way," he explains. "But as an immigrant coming to this country without any support or resources, he didn't have the opportunity to start his own business. I did, and I knew I was very fortunate."

But the music company wasn't scaling. They tried pivoting to personalized ringtones as the mobile phone market exploded in North America, Europe, and Asia. Ned and his partners met with several angel investors but couldn't convince anyone to fund the business.

Ned began to wonder if there was something else he could do, something with more long-term potential. Applying his energy toward products and services that made a marginal impact in the lives of customers who were already affluent wasn't especially satisfying. There had to be more he could do to truly transform people's lives, either in the U.S. or abroad.

That's when Ned discovered the emerging sphere of social entrepreneurship, or for-profit businesses that are driven by the triple bottom line of positive financial, social, and environmental outcomes. It was the perfect marriage of all the things he was most passionate about: business, technology, and making a positive impact. But how to begin pursuing social entrepreneurship?

A few months later, in a moment of prayer, Ned heard a clear divine message: Apply to business school. That's where he would learn the knowledge and skills he needed to scale up a company. That's where he would access the resources and connections

An early passion of Ned's was music, especially the guitar and the piano

required to build something that would truly impact families in need.

After doing some research, Ned found that Stanford University, the alma mater in his backyard, had one of the world's strongest social entrepreneurship programs. With razor-sharp clarity, he knew that was exactly where he was supposed to be.

Stanford was the only business school he applied to. There was no backup plan.

When Ned received the congratulatory call from the GSB dean of admissions, it seemed like a confirmation that everything in his life had been leading to this moment. He handed off the ringtone company to his business partner, and, shortly after marrying, moved with his wife, Dorcas, to a small apartment within biking distance of Stanford in the fall of 2005. He was prepared to dedicate everything he had to his MBA program. If he was truly going to start a high-impact company, he had to make the most of the two years he had at the business school.

From the moment he first browsed the course catalog, Ned had identified Entrepreneurial Design for Extreme Affordability as the most essential class he had to take. This would be the best course to help him understand how to develop technology-based solutions that addressed significant social challenges. But the yearlong class only had a limited number of spots. Ned applied for the class—and didn't get in. Suddenly, things weren't going according to plan.

Most of the students in the class were second-year MBA students. But Ned had already decided to focus on learning and finding business partners during his first year. In his second year, he planned to lay the groundwork for a business he could launch when he graduated. But this wasn't possible if he couldn't join the Extreme Affordability class in his first year.

So, Ned decided not to take no for an answer. On the first day of the class, he showed up, even though his name wasn't on the roster. He asked the professors if he could sit in on the class. A little baffled, they agreed. The next class, Ned came again. For weeks, he continued to attend a class he wasn't supposed to be a part of. "I just kept showing up," Ned says, laughing. "Eventually someone dropped out of the class, and they let me officially join."

The focus of the class—applying the best product design principles, especially human-centered design, to develop solutions for the 2.7 billion people who live on less than US$2.50 per day—resonated deeply with Ned. The class was partnering with an NGO in Myanmar, called Proximity Design, to develop products based on the needs and desires articulated by Burmese families. This helped Ned understand that he could probably have the greatest impact if he started a company that worked in emerging markets and developing countries, where populations had been deeply underserved for far too long.

While Ned didn't know precisely what kind of company he wanted to start, he had learned in his previous start-up experiences that business partners often mattered more than the business idea itself. In the few short weeks since arriving at Stanford, Ned had already determined that Sam Goldman, with his passion and extensive in-the-field experience, was someone he would like to work with. "I wanted to work with someone who wasn't just going to talk about doing something, but would actually *do* something after business school," Ned recalled. "And I knew Sam was going to do something."

In the second semester of the class, the students were asked to divide into groups that would design and prototype a product solution for the NGO in Myanmar. The students were given few instructions aside from grouping together by interest and having a mix of business and engineering students. Because the NGO was particularly interested in water-related solutions, most of the students formed groups around water needs.

Ignoring the others, Ned made a beeline for Sam, who, at that time, had multiple piercings and dressed unlike anyone else in their business school cohort. Sam was on an entirely different wavelength from the rest of the class. He had created a sign that read, "LIGHT & POWER," which sounded like as good of an area as any to Ned. The two began talking, and were soon joined by three other students—two engineers and another business student—who were looking for something a little different.

India: A Partner in Early Field Research

Co-founder Erica Estrada-Liou first encountered Kamla Devy during one of her early research trips to India. "Most Indian women I met were very quiet, but she was clearly the boss of her family," Erica remembers with a laugh. She gave Kamla an early Nova prototype to use and observed how it affected her morning activities.

Over the course of two days, the women spent hours together. "Kamla was always so happy to see me. She was really chatty and had a great spirit." Erica shadowed Kamla as she woke up at 4 a.m. to sweep the house and milk the buffalo, and then went on to work in the fields all day.

After using the prototype, Kamla encouraged her husband, Udayveer, to purchase a Nova. Within days, he had collected thirteen orders from his neighbors. He went on to become a village entrepreneur who sold d.light products to families in the surrounding community. This allowed him and Kamla to provide a private school education for their children.

Chapter 3

ERICA ESTRADA-LIOU

E rica Estrada-Liou's path to d.light began with a flyer posted in an elevator in the Terman Engineering Building at Stanford University. The flyer advertised a class for engineering students and business students called Entrepreneurial Design for Extreme Affordability.

By this time, Erica was finishing her undergraduate degree in mechanical engineering at Stanford University and was preparing to enter the master's program. In the previous two years, she had discovered that she loved doing hands-on projects that created real products. She had spent many hours in Stanford's Product Realization Lab, doing sandcasting, welding, and metal cutting. Now she was looking for her next challenge. The Extreme Affordability class just happened to merge two of Erica's primary interests: building products and emerging markets.

When Erica was young, her father often lived and worked abroad, managing large construction projects in other countries. She usually stayed home in Pearland, Texas (near Houston), with her mother and younger brother, but occasionally the family would travel together. Erica attended sixth grade in Venezuela and spent her summers as a high school student in Mexico.

So, when she saw the opportunity to build high-impact products for emerging markets through this class, Erica knew it was fate. "I had never thought that, as an engineer, I could make any positive impact on poverty," she says. "I was awestruck." She applied for the coveted class in the 2005-06 academic year, and was soon accepted.

The class met in a portable building just a little bigger than a shipping container, which had been built by the team of cross-disciplinary professors. Most of the furniture had been purchased from low-cost furniture retailer IKEA; a large dog that belonged to one of the instructors wandered freely around. "The atmosphere was pretty rough around the edges," Erica recalls.

During the first semester, students were asked to improve the coffee-drinking experience through creativity, human-centered design, and rapid prototyping. But it wasn't until spring break of 2006 that things got real: As part of the class, Erica and four other students traveled to Myanmar to meet with the design school's

d.light Babies Around the World

In villages in Asia and Africa, d.light lanterns have played a key role in maternal and neonatal health. Doctors, nurses, and midwives have purchased d.light solar lamps to help with deliveries.

A Burmese distributor once shared a story of a woman who experienced complications in labor. She needed to go to the hospital for an emergency procedure. But it was late at night and, without any electricity, it was too dark for medical staff to operate on her.

Fortunately, someone from her village owned an S200. Hearing about the situation, he ran home and brought the lantern to the hospital. The doctors agreed to operate. The operation was successful, and mother and baby were in good health afterwards.

On another occasion, Ned met a nurse and midwife in rural Cameroon who had delivered more than thirty babies under the light of an S250. "She couldn't stop singing its praises," Ned remembers.

NGO partner, Proximity Design, and to conduct on-the-ground customer research.

"I had spent a lot of time in Mexico, Venezuela, and Peru, but I had never seen such poverty," Erica reflects. "It was pretty shocking." After returning to her comfortable life in the U.S., Erica couldn't stop thinking about the harsh life experienced by many Burmese.

Erica and her peers were tasked with assessing the needs of Burmese families. During her time in Myanmar, she noticed that families used candles at night for light. She asked several families how much of their income went toward paying for candles, and was stunned to learn that many families spent one-third or more of their earnings on light alone.[6]

It wasn't the first time Erica had thought about energy. In her studies, she had taken several relevant classes, including fuel cells, energy systems, and advanced thermodynamics. She began to wonder if there was something that could be done to address energy needs in Myanmar.

When the Entrepreneurial Design class began again after spring break, and students were asked to form project groups around their interests, Erica gravitated toward the large butcher paper that read, "LIGHT & POWER." That's where she first began interacting with the students who would eventually become her co-founders.

"I remember talking to Sam about Benin," she says. "Sam was very vocal about his experience in Benin and really passionate about lighting being a need." She also remembers talking to Ned about his previous experience as an entrepreneur, and finding him to be "so nice and encouraging."

The newly formed team—Erica, Sam, Ned, an engineer named Xianyi Wu, and a business student named Mario Fishman— immediately began having heated debates about what solution to pursue. Mario advocated for a power system that could provide light for an entire village; the others thought it wiser to pursue smaller solutions that served individual families and homes.

Erica was impressed by everyone's passion. "I had never been on a team that cared so much about the final outcome," she recalls.

The other teams in the class were trying to address water-related challenges in Myanmar like water purification, transport, storage, and irrigation. Erica's group was distinct in their area of focus—but also in how much they struggled. "Lots of teams were ahead of us," she explains. "We were really struggling and were always doing things last minute. All of the other teams would blow us out of the water."

The team, which eventually adopted the name *d.light*, knew that hitting the right price point was essential for developing a lighting product that Burmese families could actually afford. This pushed them to experiment with all kinds of materials, from cut-up Coca-Cola cans to bamboo stems.

A breakthrough moment came, Erica recalls, when they decided to concentrate on the needs of the shopkeeper. This insight set some parameters on the potential prototype, based on the brightness and radius of illumination that an owner of a typical shop might need. The team regularly worked late into the night, creating a mock Burmese shop with materials they could find in school recycling bins, and testing out various prototypes.

With assistance from an electrical engineer and class consultant named Kurt Kuhlmann, Erica and the team finally produced a simple battery-powered light that consisted of several LEDs threaded through a red PVC pipe. She recalls that the class professors were pleasantly surprised. "No one expected us to produce anything," she says, laughing.

The simulated Burmese shop that the team created for their class project

At the end of the class, Erica was happy to be finished and to get some sleep. The team dispersed for summer vacation, with each individual taking on a different internship. And that, she was sure, was the end of the project.

In the fall of 2006, as most of the team (aside from Mario, who had already graduated) entered their second year of graduate school, Ned sent an email, asking to meet. Erica remembers Sam making the pitch to the rest of the group as they sat on the grass of the famous Stanford Oval, soaking up the warm California sun. The last prototype they made was pretty good. Could they continue to work on developing this project?

All four of them agreed to continue working on d.light. "That class showed me that what students make doesn't just sit on shelves. It gets produced, and it can get into the hands of real customers," Erica reflects.

Over the next several months, Erica focused on completing the last two quarters of her graduate program while putting long hours into d.light. She had secured a full-time position with Lockheed Martin, a leading developer of aerospace, defense, and security technologies worldwide, which was supposed to start as soon she finished her classes in March 2007.

From late 2006 to early 2007, the prototypes underwent quite a transformation. Through their ongoing field research, the d.light team had come to understand that their products had to be extremely durable, weather resistant, and allow for flexible usage. The red PVC pipe wasn't sufficient. They needed to come up with a better, more comprehensive design.

The next prototype iteration, called the ForeverBright, had larger housing to contain the circuit and a sealed-lead-acid battery. It could be solar

Erica and Ned with their final prototype for the design class

charged or AC charged, and had a large metal handle for carrying or hanging. It used a dozen white LEDs, spaced evenly in a rectangular pattern. Most of the prototypes were rectangular; a few were round. A design question that the team had to answer was which shape customers liked more.

The d.light team had maintained a relationship with Proximity Design in Myanmar, and agreed to send them twenty-five prototypes of the ForeverBright. These would be divided between randomly selected households in Myanmar and Cambodia, who would test the prototypes and provide feedback.

After a huge effort by the entire team to finish the prototypes on time, they were shipped to Southeast Asia. A couple of team members needed to follow the products into the field to collect feedback. Since Xianyi had already finished his degree, he was a logical choice to go. Erica, who had also finished her studies and developed a growing expertise in ethnography, was the other obvious choice.

But that meant delaying her start date with Lockheed Martin. She met with the man who would be her supervisor at Lockheed— who, coincidentally, was also named Ned—and asked if she could delay her start date by three months. He recognized her passion for d.light, and readily agreed.

In early May 2007, she and Xianyi began a two-month research trip to Cambodia and Myanmar. Unbeknownst to them, during that trip d.light would be kickstarted into a real company.

Erica with an off-grid family in Cambodia during a customer research trip

Chapter 4

After Xianyi Wu, who typically went by Xian, finished his third year at Carnegie Mellon University (CMU), he took a trip that changed his life. A mechanical engineering student, he had always been interested in helping people in poverty but didn't know how to connect it with his love of tinkering and building.

Then, in 2003, the Singaporean had the opportunity to spend an entire summer in the recently formed country of East Timor (also known as Timor Leste) with the Christian organization Youth With a Mission. Xian remembers flying to Díli, the capital of East Timor, and enduring a harrowing eight-hour car ride through a mountain pass with bumpy roads and wild turns around sharp corners.

He and the other young people in his team were "just plopped into a village," Xian recalls. Their mission that summer was intentionally ambiguous. Some of his teammates had medical training, so they began working in a local clinic. But what could an engineer do? Soon after arriving, Xian encountered a group of Australians who were installing solar water pumps and followed their work closely throughout the summer.

Xian worked with his teammates to develop a questionnaire for local villagers, which asked them about their lives and what resources they most wanted and needed. It was his earliest encounter with need-finding and human-centered design—though he didn't know to call them such at the time.

Everybody in the village, including the foreigners, burned kerosene oil for light at night. Xian remembers how a Timorese friend, while trying to pump-start his lamp, got hit in the eyes with kerosene. The burning liquid can cause blindness, so Xian helped his friend wash out his eyes as quickly as possible. "That was really scary," he remembers. Another day, a young child came into the medical clinic, his face covered in burns from spilled kerosene.

When Xian returned to Carnegie Mellon to finish his last year, he was more determined than ever to apply his engineering background to combatting poverty. His parents really wanted him to get a master's degree, and he saw that as an opportunity to further this goal. He was interested in staying at CMU, but then he got accepted to Stanford University's School of Engineering. His family members and his spiritual mentor encouraged him to go.

Once he made the decision, Xian became excited about a design track focused on product creation that Stanford offered. In

Xian and a YWAM colleague with a few of the Timorese
they met on their summer missions trip

particular, a class called Entrepreneurial Design for Extreme Affordability caught his eye. "As soon as I saw that class in the course catalog, I circled it and said, 'This is the one class I have to go to,'" Xian remembers. He applied for the competitive class but, like Ned, he wasn't accepted.

Xian was so sure he needed to be in the class that he decided to take a risk. He had heard that the lead professor of the class, Jim Patell, admired persistence. So, Xian decided to go to Jim's office and beg to be included in the class. The first two times Xian went, Jim wasn't there. The hallway of the business school staff building was dark and eerily quiet, and Xian nearly lost his nerve.

On Xian's third visit, Jim was in his office. Xian heard a muffled "come in" after knocking on the door. He opened the door, entered the office, and pled his case. Jim listened without saying anything. Then he replied gruffly, "Okay, well, I guess we'll let you in."

Without Xian, d.light might never have been *d.light*. He and his team members in the class had to come up with a project name. Despite constant brainstorming, they couldn't think of a name that everyone liked.

Then, one night, Xian was in bed, reading his Bible. He came across Psalm 37:4. "Delight yourself in the Lord, and he will give you the desires of your heart," the verse reads in the English Standard Version. Right away, Xian knew what the project should be called. The team loved the name, as it captured the emotion— delight—that they wanted customers to experience when encountering their product. They spelled it *d.light* as a nod to the nickname for Stanford's design school, d.school.

Like Erica, Xian remembers how the team struggled throughout the school term. "We had no clue what we were doing," he recalls. Somehow their final product came together just days before the end of the class. Fortunately, the professors loved their simple PVC pipe and LED prototype.

In the fall of 2006, when the four remaining team members met to consider pursuing d.light outside of class, Xian was faced with a serious dilemma. He was scheduled to graduate at the end of 2006, a semester early. As a foreign student, the clock began ticking on Xian's American visa as soon as he finished school. The US government gives foreign students twelve months to find a job and an employer who is willing to sponsor them for a work visa.

Xian had already used three of those months for a summer internship at Apple in 2006. He only had nine months of his visa left. He was also weighed down by the fact that his parents had spent quite a bit of money to send him to university in the U.S., with the hope that he could get a good-paying job.

None of these factors supported the idea of joining a start-up that had no money and wasn't even yet a legal entity. Xian loved d.light, but, in many ways, it didn't make sense for him.

Then, at the very end of 2006, he attended Urbana, an international student missions conference organized by InterVarsity Christian Fellowship. For the first time in its sixty-year history, the conference offered a track of lectures and seminars on the topic of

New Kerenga, India: The First d.light Village

In 2008, d.light conducted a pilot with micro-finance organization Beyond Solar in three villages in the Koraput district of southern Odisha. The villages were made up of extremely low-income households that had an average monthly income of less than US$13 and relied exclusively on kerosene for light. With a small down payment and affordable weekly installments, families were given the option to purchase a Nova.

Across the three villages of Puki, Ganjei Prada, and New Kerenga, 72 percent of families purchased a Nova. They reported saving about US$3 a month on kerosene costs, and were also able to work more, which increased their monthly income to as high as US$18.

In New Kerenga, 100 percent of families decided to purchase a Nova, making it the first village in the world lit completely by d.light lanterns.

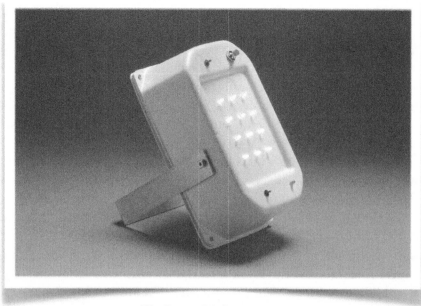

The ForeverBright prototype

business as mission. While at the conference, Xian became very clear that d.light was his next step. "I felt it was the right thing for me," he explains. He could only stay in the country for another nine months; he wasn't going to receive any salary; he didn't even have a place to live. Yet Xian was absolutely confident that d.light was his calling.

For the first half of 2007, Xian relied on friends to house him. He would sleep on a friend's couch for three to four weeks at a time and then, conscious of not burdening anyone too much, he would pack his suitcases and two guitars into his car and move on to the next friend's couch.

Fortunately, d.light was beginning to take shape, primarily by relying on the ample resources of Stanford University. "Sam is a hustler," Xian explains. Sam convinced Stanford faculty to provide d.light with a small office space and ongoing access to the student machine shop so they could build prototypes. Knowing Xian's difficult situation, Sam also got Stanford to pay him a small stipend to cover basic living costs.

As Sam, Ned, and Erica juggled their classes with d.light, Xian was the only person working exclusively on the project. It was a season of exceptionally hard work, during which he built d.light's first website and took the lead in designing and creating the twenty-five prototypes of the ForeverBright that would be sent to Myanmar and Cambodia for field testing.

Xian had to share the Stanford machine shop with students and work around the shop's irregular hours. As the deadline neared to send the prototypes to Southeast Asia, he had to double his efforts to manually form, cut, and build the plastic housing for each individual prototype. "For a week, as long as the machine shop was open, I would be there," he remembers. Each night, at the end of a long day, he would reek of machine oil when he returned to whichever dorm room or apartment he was temporarily staying in.

The push to finish those prototypes on time culminated in an all-night, all-hands effort. Every member of the d.light team, plus their significant others and a volunteer electrical engineer named Gabriel Risk, stayed up until 4 a.m., soldering circuit boards and assembling the units. They were shipped off to Myanmar and Cambodia that morning, so that users would have time to use the prototypes before Xian and Erica arrived to do testing.

Once in Cambodia and Myanmar, Xian and Erica worked extremely long days with no breaks in between, traveling to various villages and interviewing users in sweltering conditions.

While in Cambodia, the two were given desk space in an NGO's office that was no more than a converted shipping container. One day at the end of May 2007, Xian and Erica returned to the office from yet another long day of field research. "We were hot, sticky, and tired," Xian remembers. He was too exhausted to check his email, but Erica fired up her computer and opened her inbox. A moment later, she said, "What?" in an incredulous voice.

"What is it?" Xian asked.

Erica showed him an email from Ned, with no subject line and no text. All it had was a photo of an oversize US$250,000 check, made out to d.light.

Xian with children in Cambodia in May 2007

Chapter 5

For as long as he can remember, Gabriel Risk wanted to be an engineer. He had always loved building things and putting things together. As a native of San Francisco, he conveniently lived right next to some of the top engineering universities in the country. He earned electrical engineering degrees from the University of California, Berkeley, as an undergraduate, and then from Stanford University as a graduate student.

After finishing school, Gabe went to work for Sun Microsystems, helping to build huge, million-dollar computer servers for corporations. Then, in the fall of 2005, his wife, Diana, started her first year as a student at the Stanford Graduate School of Business.

Throughout her time at Stanford, Diana liked to regularly invite business school classmates over for dinner. In the fall of 2006, at the start of her second year, she invited Sam Goldman to the small apartment that she and Gabe shared.

Gabe remembers making small talk with Sam, asking about his classes. Sam replied that most of his classes weren't out of the ordinary, but there was one class, called Entrepreneurial Design for Extreme Affordability, that he was really excited about.

"We've made this light, and it could really help a lot of people," Sam explained enthusiastically. Then he paused. "But it's weird. It doesn't always work." The LED light that he and his teammates were trying to build sometimes worked exactly as expected when they connected it to a battery. Other times, the LEDs would flash really brightly and then go off.

Liangshan District, China: Bringing Laughter and Singing to Mountain Villages

d.light partnered with the Jet Li Foundation in 2009-10 to provide lamps to off-grid villages in the mountain regions of Liangshan District, Sichuan Province. In an initial pilot, seventy-five families of the Yi ethnic minority were provided a subsidized Nova Mobile.

Households that received the lights were able to save, on average, more than US$20 a month in energy costs. Children increased their study time by more than an hour each night, and activities such as outdoor work and leisure activities increased significantly. A local NGO used the lights to start a night school to teach the villagers Mandarin, hygiene, and life skills.

Through the partnership, more than 21,000 Yi families received a solar lamp. One villager shared, "Finally, our small mountain village has light at night! Now we are able to reap our corn, feed our cows, read, and study at night. Our villages will never again experience the pitch-black night. Instead, in the newly opened night school, there is laughter and singing for all the mountains to hear."

This was an engineering problem that Gabe couldn't ignore. "Can you draw me the circuit you're using?" he asked Sam.

Sam drew a simple diagram, showing that the device wasn't much more than LEDs connected to a battery.

Gabe knew right away what was wrong. "You have the wrong circuit. You need a resistor in there. Otherwise, it's not going to work."

"Oh, really?" Sam asked. "What's a resistor?"

Gabe explained how the resistor could regulate electrical current, and provided recommendations for how to design the circuit. What he didn't know yet was that Sam was an expert hustler, and he was about to rope Gabe into his class project-turned-business.

"Well, we could do it ourselves," Sam began slowly. "Or, you could just come work with us in the afternoons, after we finish our classes. You're underworked and looking for something to do anyways, right?"

It was true. Sun Microsystems, which would be acquired by and fully absorbed into Oracle Corporation less than four years later, was already in trouble.[7] Layoffs were happening every year, and morale was low. Gabe recalls how every project would go over time and over budget. His team regularly completed their work on time, but then they were forced to wait for other teams to catch up. As a result, he had a lot of downtime and was looking to fill it with something else that engaged and challenged him.

Two days after dinner with Sam, Gabe went to the design school at Stanford to meet Ned, Xian, and Erica for the first time. He recalls being impressed with the energy of the group. They were clearly having fun and enjoying one another's company, despite their long odds of success. It was exactly what Gabe was looking for.

"That was my mantra at the time," Gabe explains. "Take on a project that no one else wants to tackle." He began working on the circuit that would go into the second iteration of the ForeverBright.

At the time, the d.light team still hadn't determined whether the lights should be primarily solar powered or AC powered. While conducting field research in Myanmar, they had found that a surprising number of households had access to a generator, usually in the town closest to their village. If customers could occasionally use a generator to charge the battery with AC electricity, AC charging could be a critical feature to include.

Gabe remembers trying to design a circuit that could handle the inconsistent surges of power that generators often produce while also optimizing available AC power for super-fast charging —and including the option for solar charging. It wasn't easy trying to include all these features into a very low-cost circuit.

d.light didn't yet have an office at the time, so Gabe turned his kitchen table into a lab bench. "We didn't have a big apartment," he recalls. "The kitchen was the largest part, and d.light

Gabe works on the ForeverBright circuit in his kitchen

had claimed it." Every inch of the table was covered with LEDs, experimental circuit boards, and a soldering station. Occasionally, if he and Diana had guests over for dinner, he would pack everything up into a box and hide it away in the basement so there would be a place to eat.

As d.light progressed, Gabe dedicated all of his spare time to the project. Fortunately, Gabe's manager and team at Sun were incredibly supportive. When Gabe asked for permission to pursue d.light while still working for Sun, his manager granted it without hesitation. The arrangement worked quite well, allowing Gabe to focus on building d.light while still supporting his team at Sun.

As Gabe and Xian worked hard to produce the twenty-five prototypes that would eventually go to Myanmar and Cambodia, and Erica focused on customer research, Sam and Ned began entering d.light into business plan competitions.

"The whole pitch was a PowerPoint presentation with no words, just beautiful pictures," Gabe remembers. The presentation included photos of kerosene lamps and consumers that the team had met during their field research. Despite its simplicity, the pitch was extremely compelling, and Sam and Ned began winning a few thousand dollars here and there from various competitions.

But the competition that remains the most vivid in Gabe's memory is the one that d.light didn't win. In the spring of 2007, they entered the Global Social Venture Competition (GSVC), hosted at the Haas School of Business at the University of California, Berkeley, now one of the most well-known business plan competitions for social enterprises. The d.light team was determined to take home the first prize of US$25,000.

The GSVC connected d.light with a business mentor, a long-time supply chain expert named John Schram who had overseen apparel manufacturing in China with Sears and Levi Strauss. Under John's guidance, Sam and Ned completely revamped the d.light business plan and broadened their market beyond Myanmar to include much of South and Southeast Asia. They also, for the first time, firmly categorized themselves as a for-profit company that would seek out venture capital funding. In addition, they decided to set a seemingly impossible goal, both to motivate themselves but also to signal to investors that they were very serious about growing a global company: they wanted to reach 11 million households by the year 2012.

In the business plan that was submitted to the GSVC, they wrote: "Our vision is to build a light and power brand for BOP [base-of-the-pyramid] customers. d.light design will be the leading supplier of branded affordable household LED light and power solutions to rural BOP customers globally, measured by units sold

Gabe tests a circuit design at the Stanford d.school

and percent of households recommending products to friends and family."[8]

"We spent weeks preparing for the GSVC," Ned remembers. "That felt like the first real pitch we ever made. We were really nervous."

Despite their efforts, d.light ended up tying for second place, while San Francisco-based Revolution Foods, which provides healthy meals to public schools in low-income neighborhoods in the U.S., won. The three second-place winners split the US$15,000 prize, with each receiving US$5,000. The next day, d.light was awarded the social impact assessment prize for an additional US$5,000.

All five members of the team had attended the event, and, based on the strength of Sam and Ned's pitch, they really thought they had a shot at winning. They were extremely disappointed to walk away with only US$10,000. Later that night, the team bonded over their frustration and became even more determined to grow the company into a successful business. "We're going to do this," they told one another. "We're going to do what they're saying can't be done."

As Gabe remembers it, "That was the night that d.light became a real company."

A few weeks later, Sam and Ned entered d.light into the Draper Fisher Jurvetson Venture Challenge, the competition that would end up changing everything.

The founding team at the 2007 Global Social Venture Competition

Chapter 6

A few months before the GSVC, at the end of 2006, Sam and Ned had traveled to Myanmar for the first time to meet potential customers and better understand the market. They encountered one woman, a brick maker and mother named Mi-Ya, who tearfully begged to buy a very simple prototype—no more than a string of LEDs attached to a battery and a solar panel— from them. Her emotional response, along with the great need they saw throughout Myanmar, furthered their motivation to build a real product that they could distribute to off-grid families.

In order to do that, though, they needed funding. Sam and Ned calculated that a relatively modest US$200,000 could provide a livable income for the founders and launch the product in Myanmar. At first, they ruled out venture capitalists, whom they believed would never fund a social enterprise. That left two routes to funding, both of which required intensive labor and offered lower returns: angel investors and business plan competitions.

During the first five months of 2007, as they also managed their heavy class loads, Sam and Ned pitched to at least a dozen angel investors. None of them were enthusiastic. Many didn't even believe d.light could be a viable business.

"You have to remember that this was 2007," Sam explains. "No one really understood social enterprise yet. You were either a nonprofit that did social good or you were a for-profit that had a separate foundation or corporate social responsibility arm."

They received the harshest feedback from the lead investor of a well-respected angel investor forum in the San Francisco Bay Area. She argued that d.light should target developed markets and use a portion of its revenue to serve base-of-the-pyramid families. When Sam and Ned respectfully disagreed, she became even more forthcoming. "I know about businesses," she insisted. "You two seem like nice guys, but I have to tell you, you will fail. I'm sure of it."

India: A Young Girl's Life Changed

During the first year of d.light operations in India, special projects manager Aarthi Jambhulka met a young village girl who was struggling. "She had almost no future because no one wanted to marry her, and there was no electricity in the house, so she couldn't study," Aarthi remembers.

Then the girl's family purchased a Nova. When Aarthi followed up with them, she learned that, thanks to having light, the girl had been able to continue her studies and even finished secondary school.

"It was a life that was impacted and changed," says Aarthi.

The d.light team found a much better response from several Stanford-affiliated business leaders. That semester Sam approached two business legends, Michael Marks and Michael Dearing, who happened to be his professors, to ask for advice. They readily agreed to help. Marks answered their questions about supply chain management, while Dearing shared his expertise in innovative organizational structures. Even more importantly, both men expressed interest in staying informed about the nascent social venture—and eventually offered angel investment if Sam and Ned could raise other funding on their own. Tom Bird, an angel investor whom Ned had met after he spoke in one of Ned's classes, also agreed to invest after d.light had secured other funding.

With limited success among angel investors, the d.light team turned to business plan competitions. The first competition that d.light entered was the Charles River Entrepreneur Idol competition, which took place at the Stanford business school. The competition asked students to make a sixty-second pitch to the panel of judges. The best pitch would win US$1,000.

Based on availability, Ned was tasked with the pitch. He practiced and practiced, timing his speech to the second to make the most compelling pitch possible within the time limit. He also had a very powerful prop: a blue kerosene lantern, brought back by Sam's dad after a business trip to Nigeria.

Right before it was Ned's turn to present to the judges, he lit the lamp. It began to spew dark, noxious plumes of gas into the Stanford classroom. "This is what 1.3 billion people in the world use for light at night every day," he began. He could see by the wide eyes of the judges and audience members that he had fully captured their attention. An hour later, the $1,000 prize was awarded to Ned and d.light.

But that was nowhere near enough. After the disappointment of losing the GSVC, Sam and Ned began to search more broadly for other business plan competitions. One evening, Sam received an email from a family friend about a business plan competition hosted by venture capital firm Draper Fisher Jurvetson. DFJ, headquartered only a few miles away from Stanford, was known for funding huge successes like Baidu, Skype, and Twitter, and would later go on to fund SpaceX and Tesla.

*Ned, Sam, and Erica with the kerosene lantern that helped them
win multiple business plan competitions*

Any business plan that had placed first in a university-level competition in the U.S. was eligible for DFJ's competition. The winner would receive a whopping US$250,000. The second-place prize? Nothing.

Sam was pretty sure DFJ would never want to fund a social enterprise. Besides, d.light wasn't even eligible for the competition. They'd placed second at the GSVC, and Stanford's business plan competition wouldn't take place until the week after the DFJ Venture Challenge. He deleted the email.

But the competition—and its immense prize money—stayed in the back of his mind. A few days later, he pulled the email out of his deleted folder and forwarded it to Ned on the off chance that his business partner could make something of it.

When Ned saw the email, he read it differently: d.light met most of the eligibility criteria, except for the small matter of winning a business plan competition that hadn't yet taken place. So he called up a junior associate at DFJ and asked her for advice. "I told her about d.light and asked her what she thought we needed to do to win," he explains. "I asked her how we could make a compelling pitch. She gave some great advice. And then I said, 'By the way, our school's business plan competition hasn't happened yet, but we're pretty sure we're going to win it. So can we still participate?' Right away, she said, 'Sure, no problem.'"

The bigger challenge was actually finding time to prepare for the competition. Sam and Ned were still full-time students who had hours of homework to complete each night.

It was only very late on the evening of May 30, 2007, that Ned remembered the DFJ competition was the following morning. He called Sam at midnight to remind him. They considered not participating but decided they might as well. They had done so many pitches by then that they could quickly put together the five-minute presentation required for the competition. They agreed to meet early the next morning so they could arrive at the Draper Fisher Jurvetson offices by 8 a.m.

That morning, Ned donned the only nice blazer he owned. Sam didn't have a suit and had to borrow one from a classmate. The two students, who had spent more time in off-grid villages than investor offices, felt terribly out of place in the upscale DFJ headquarters. As soon as the other presentations started, they began to sweat even more.

"We knew we were in trouble," Sam remembers. "Every single presentation was amazing. The companies were unbelievable. Everyone had a game-changing idea that involved more extensive IP [intellectual property] and faster returns. We had no chance. But we did have that kerosene lantern."

Even with the kerosene lantern's dramatic black smoke, they weren't sure they could win over the panel of judges. One of the judges, a well-known Silicon Valley investor, didn't hide his disdain for their social mission. As soon as they began discussing the potential social impact of d.light, he rolled his eyes.

When all the presentations had concluded, it was announced that lunch would be served while the judges deliberated. Someone with a DFJ badge approached Sam and Ned as they headed toward the buffet table. "Can I have your USB stick?" he asked.

"What?" they replied, not understanding.

"For your next presentation," he explained patiently. "In case you get selected as a finalist."

They looked at each other. Neither of them had read the email announcement as closely as they should have. They had assumed that the second-round presentation was exactly the same as the first. Obviously, they were wrong.

"Give us a minute," Sam replied, thinking quickly. "We'll get it to you soon."

He and Ned dashed out of the room, down the hall, and into the parking lot as quickly as their formalwear could carry them. They quickly added a few more slides to their PowerPoint presentation and strategized on how to expand their content.

They spent the entire lunch break practicing their new presentation. The finalists wouldn't be announced until after lunch, but they thought it wise to be prepared. As their peers enjoyed canapés, Sam made his pitch to a tree and Ned practiced while walking laps around his car.

When they reentered the room, they were hungry but wired on coffee and adrenaline. One of the judges stood up to announce the five finalists. After the fourth finalist was named, Sam and Ned assumed they hadn't made it to the next round. They were resigned to having made a good effort.

But then they heard it: d.light was the fifth finalist and would be the first team to present again.

Stunned, the co-founders returned before the audience and the skeptical judges. But something clicked in that moment, and Sam and Ned found themselves giving the presentation of their lives.

"That's still one of the best pitches we've ever given. Everything went well," Ned reflects. "And that burning kerosene lantern was as effective as ever."

Their elation dimmed, however, as the other finalists also gave stellar presentations. But the co-founders had given it their all. After the judges deliberated, it was, fittingly, the initially skeptical investor who stood up to announce the results of the competition. "Let there d.light!" he declared.

That actual moment has become a bit fuzzy for both Sam and Ned, who remember little more than feeling shock and jubilation. They somehow ended up at the front of the room. Someone handed them an oversize check that, unbelievably, had both *d.light* and $250,000 on it, while someone else took their picture. It was an incredible moment.

"I felt like I had won the Super Bowl," Sam says. "It was one of the best moments of my life."

It was Ned's idea to send the photo of the check, uncaptioned and with no subject line, to Xian and Erica in Cambodia. Thinking it couldn't possibly be real, the two engineers went to sleep after seeing the email and didn't call until the following day. "What was that all about?" they asked Ned. "Is that a joke?"

"Nope," Ned replied happily. "It's real. We won $250,000."

Xian and Erica were stunned. "I knew suddenly everything was different now," Xian remembers.

Sam and Ned right after being handed the winning prize for the DFJ competition

Chapter 7

No one could say that d.light was only an idea or school project now, and the founders were ready to fully commit. Erica officially turned down her Lockheed Martin job. Sam said no to a job with the sustainability group within corporate giant Walmart, while Ned refused an offer from Google. The three of them, plus Xian, could finally begin to receive some form of salary. Gabe remained on the payroll of Sun Microsystems, even as his commitment to d.light reached—and sometimes surpassed—full time.

Just after winning the DFJ competition, the team moved ahead with officially incorporating the business and establishing job titles for each member of the team. Sam was the chief executive officer, Ned the president, and Gabe the chief technology officer. Xian headed up product development and Erica led customer research.

Another priority for the d.light team was to secure an actual office rather than rely on Stanford or Gabe's kitchen table. The DFJ competition prize included a year's worth of subsidized office space in a co-working building in Sunnyvale, a city about ten miles south of Stanford University.

But from the first day they moved into the co-working space, the founders were pretty sure it wasn't going to work. "We show up with drills, prototypes, soldering irons, but the office building turned out to be full of cubicles," Erica remembers. Every other start-up seemed to be comprised of only people and computers; no one else needed an engineering lab. Then the d.light team discovered that, even with DFJ's subsidy, the office space would still cost them about US$700 a month in utilities and other fees.

They conferred and immediately agreed that they needed another space. Sam and Ned went back to DFJ, asking if d.light could have the cash value of the office subsidy instead. The VC firm agreed to give them an additional US$9,000 on top of the US$250,000 they had already provided.

The founders went on the classified listing website Craigslist, searching for various spaces near Stanford. They found an office space in a quiet cul-de-sac in the neighboring city of Mountain View for an even lower rent than the subsidized co-working space. The building's owner, who also happened to be a Stanford GSB alumnus, was offering the approximately 370-square-foot space at a below-market rate for two reasons: the space was oddly shaped, with one large triangular room and a smaller square room, and the building was scheduled to be demolished by the city in a few years. But the space was more than enough for the d.light team, and they happily signed the lease.

Erica in the first official d.light office in Mountain View, California

Five days after moving all their prototypes and engineering tools into the Sunnyvale co-working space, the d.light team moved it all again. They tried to turn the Mountain View office into a fun space on a limited budget, painting the walls bright yellow, and adding bean bags for seating and a punching bag for stress relief. Xian set up a basketball net in the cul-de-sac of the street in case they needed to release some energy outdoors.

The other half of the building was occupied by a cleaning service. "As we showed up to work in the morning, they would leave with vacuum cleaners and cleaning supplies," Erica recalls. The team spent many long days and nights there, continuing to develop their first products, conduct research, and engage in fundraising.

With more than a quarter million dollars in convertible notes committed, Ned and Sam renewed and expanded their search for investment with far more momentum. A Stanford business school professor had once told them that the first $250,000 was always the hardest to raise. If they could get that, then the money would begin coming far more easily. He would prove to be correct.

After they won Stanford's social business plan competition (netting another US$10,000) and received firm commitments from angel investors Michael Marks, Michael Deering, and Tom Bird, other investors began paying much more attention to the tiny start-up called d.light. Ned had breakfast with Bill Reichert, a managing partner at Garage Technology Ventures, whom he had met through his previous start-ups. He told Bill about d.light, including their mission, strategy, and funding situation. By the end of the breakfast, before an official ask was even made, Bill said, "We'll match what DFJ put in." Ned was stunned. He'd never had the experience of raising funding so easily.

Shortly after, impact investment fund Gray Matters Capital also agreed to provide funding. The d.light team had met managing partner Steve Hardgrave at the Global Social Venture Competition. At that time, Steve had already expressed interest in investing in d.light, but it took a few months for him to get all the necessary approvals.

By this time, the team had firmly shifted away from Myanmar and made India their first target market, both because of its size and its inherent challenges. "Every stat showed that India was the largest off-grid market in the world," Sam explains. "Our belief from the get-go was that customers in India were so demanding of both the feature set they wanted and the extremely low price point they would pay that if we could crack it in India, we could do it in any market." In particular, they wanted to start in the states of Uttar Pradesh and Bihar, which both had huge off-grid populations. The d.light team hoped that this strategy would allow them to scale quickly and become financially sustainable.

Focusing on India helped win over additional investors. Nexus Venture Partners, a venture capital firm with headquarters in both India and Silicon Valley, expressed interest in providing funding—on one condition. They wanted Indian conglomerate Mahindra to invest with them because Mahindra understood rural farmers and could provide a key distribution network. But the d.light team would have to convince Mahindra to join the seed round. If Mahindra came in, then Nexus would as well.

Helping Human-Animal Relations

d.light's solar lanterns have played a surprisingly helpful role with animals. Bala Suleman, who lives in a town near Kano, Nigeria, used the S10 to provide light for his chickens. Their monthly production immediately jumped from 10-15 eggs per chicken per month to 30 eggs per chicken per month. This increased Bala's income, which then allowed him to purchase six more d.light lanterns.

Many customers in Asia and Africa have also reported using d.light lamps to ward off wild animals that might harm their fields or livestock, such as elephants and lions. Having bright light at night also protects families from snake bites, which kill more than 100,000 people each year and lead to permanent disabilities in hundreds of thousands more.

Sam and Ned study batteries collected from Myanmar

As they negotiated with Nexus and Mahindra, Sam and Ned were becoming increasingly concerned that their investment pool was skewing toward profit-driven venture capitalists. They knew they needed investors and board members who valued the social impact of the company as much as financial returns. The two had been courting Acumen, one of the world's leading impact investors, for several months. Acumen and its founder, Jacqueline Novogratz, liked what d.light was doing but were hesitant to invest because the start-up was so early stage. In addition, Acumen had never invested in an energy company before. "We pursued them very heavily because they were impact focused and mission aligned," Ned recalls. "But we were a weird investment for them. We didn't fit any of their criteria, and we knew it would be an experiment for them."

The co-founders wanted Acumen so badly that they were willing to do almost anything to win them over. One day, in the summer of 2007, Sam was riding to work when he turned his bike onto a small bridge. A cyclist coming from the other direction accidentally clipped him. Sam was thrown off his bike and landed hard on the pavement. One of his arms was in excruciating pain; he worried that it might be broken and wondered how he could get himself to the hospital.

Then his phone rang. It was Raj Kundra, one of the partners from Acumen, with further questions about d.light's financial models. Noticing that Sam sounded strangely out of breath, he asked, "Is this a good time?"

Sam admitted that he had just gotten into a bike accident. "I'm fine," he lied. "We can talk now." Dragging himself to the side of the bridge, he decided that going to the hospital could wait; Acumen could not. Raj sounded suitably impressed with Sam's dedication, and then launched into his questions.

The team's persistence paid off. By the end of August, Acumen had officially committed as the fourth major investor for d.light. Nexus and Mahindra added their funds in October, resulting in seed funding that totaled US$1.6 million.

It was time to begin building a real company.

Chapter 8

A CHINA EDUCATION

A s soon as d.light received its seed funding and could begin scaling, they prioritized product design and manufacturing. As brighter, more energy-efficient LEDs became available, the ForeverBright had morphed into a prism-shaped lantern with a wide plastic handle and a single LED. The founders called it the Nova, after the astronomical term for a brightening star, and hoped to launch it as the first official d.light product.

The question of where to manufacture the Nova, however, was a tricky one. The team considered doing a first run in the U.S., but the cost of purchasing the aluminum tool for production was prohibitively high.

They looked to India, as it would have been ideal to have production and sales in the same country. But no matter whom they spoke with or which factory they researched, the costs for manufacturing electronics in India were too high. The only chance d.light had of succeeding was if its products were actually affordable for base-of-the-pyramid customers.

After recommendations from several advisers, in mid-2007 the team began looking seriously at China. The city of Shenzhen, in the Pearl River Delta region, was already known as a leading producer of electronics, exporting as much as 90 percent of the world's

One of several initial models of the Nova, which was produced in blue, orange, and red

consumer electronics.[9] Contract manufacturers in the Shenzhen area produced some of the world's most sophisticated electronics, including laptops, cameras, and smartphones. And they knew how to do it cost effectively.

But finding the right contract manufacturer wasn't going to be easy. Not only did d.light need a factory that could build high-quality units at a low price, they also needed someone willing to work with a small, unknown American company that was producing minimal volumes.

In August 2007, Ned, Xian, and Gabe began traveling regularly to Shenzhen to meet with potential manufacturers. They arrived with a list of recommended firms gleaned from mentors, advisers, and investors with production experience in China. Xian remembers how they would evaluate three firms on the list at a time. When those didn't work out, they would move on to the next three. "It was the start of an education," he recalls.

"It was a big learning experience for everyone in dealing with China," Gabe agrees. "Everything from the culture, the food, the relationships with contract manufacturers—we learned how difficult that was to get right, how difficult it was to communicate."

They met with toy manufacturers and plastic manufacturers. They met with lamp producers and watch producers. But without any previous context, it was difficult for the d.light team to know how to evaluate these firms. Were they trustworthy? Were they quoting reasonable prices? Were their quality standards high enough? Were the working conditions good? Could they be trusted to protect d.light's designs and intellectual property?

To make things more difficult, Xian was the only member of the d.light team who spoke Mandarin—and his conversational abilities were limited at best. He remembers one meeting with a manufacturer during which they began throwing out contract terms in Chinese. It was suddenly incumbent upon Xian to negotiate on behalf of d.light. But he had no idea what to say or how to say it. "It was very stressful," he recalls. Fortunately, more often than not, the Chinese firms had at least one employee who spoke a little English, so they were able to manage some degree of communication.

The founders leased a modest three-bedroom apartment in the LuoHu district of Shenzhen, near the Hong Kong border, and stayed there when they visited China. The faucet in the kitchen sink would spew water straight up toward the ceiling. Whenever they hung laundry on the balcony, it would become covered in coal dust from nearby factories. Gabe remembers subsisting almost entirely on noodles from a small restaurant around the corner and a few snacks from a nearby supermarket. Since he couldn't speak any Mandarin, that was pretty much the only food he knew how to buy.

The apartment also served as an office and was full of batteries, LEDs, circuit boards, and plastic housing. Gabe and Xian were constantly running product tests in various rooms of the apartment —perhaps not the wisest thing to do in a residential high-rise.

Ned remembers being woken by his alarm one morning in the apartment. When he reached over to turn off the alarm, he knocked over a battery, which immediately shorted and set the nearby curtains on fire. "My first thought was, 'I don't know how to say *fire* in Chinese,'" he recalls. "I didn't know whom to ask for help or how to ask for help. I realized I was the only one who could put out the fire." Acting fast, Ned grabbed his blanket and managed to smother the fire.

After that, the engineers were careful to locate their prototypes a little further away from the curtains.

In the fall of 2007, Ned was introduced to a businessman from Hong Kong who enthusiastically recommended a manufacturing firm in Shenzhen. He told Ned that the owner of the firm, a man named David, was a person of very high integrity. "If I gave David $100,000 to keep for me, and told him I'd come collect it in ten years," the man explained, "I know he would keep every single cent safe until I came back, and then give me the money back with interest." Ned was impressed, and immediately contacted David to begin producing the Nova.

But while David and his team were extremely trustworthy and could produce quality units, they had trouble reaching a low enough price point to make the Nova widely affordable. "We were always disappointed at the pricing," Gabe remembers, "but it was the best we could do at the time." The d.light team had been aiming for a product that cost between US$5 to $10, but the Nova would have to retail at more than US$30.

Kanakapura, India: Boosting Student Performance

In 2010, Indian NGO Sikshana Foundation provided d.light Kirans to 84 tenth standard students in Kanakapura, Ramanagara district, in the state of Karnataka. Families in the district had extremely low incomes and were subject to frequent power cuts. When there was no electricity and households had used up their kerosene ration, students were not able to study and their performance at school suffered.

Two months before a major national exam, these 84 students were lent a Kiran. They reported an immediate increase in their study time by two to three hours per night. Eighty-two percent of them passed the exam and earned certificates, a significant increase from the district average of 67 percent.

So the co-founders tried another strategy. Instead of working with a contract manufacturer that understood quality but not cost-efficiency, they wanted to try a factory that knew how to produce lights at a low cost and would be willing to partner with d.light to improve their quality. They found a light manufacturer in Shenzhen that already produced a CFL tube light and was willing to work with d.light. The firm had friendly, collaborative managers, and quoted exceptionally good terms for them.

After the deal had been agreed to, Gabe predicted, "In six months, we're going to say this was either the very best decision or the very worst decision. There won't be anything in between."

He would turn out to be exactly right. In six months, they clearly knew that this had been a terrible decision.

The new contractor was asked to produce two additional products that would launch with the Nova: a desk lamp called the Comet, and an emergency light called the Vega. The Comet had a bendable gooseneck and came in multiple colors, with solar and AC charging options. The AC-charged Vega was rectangular and had a bright CFL tube light.

The Comet came in three different models: AC-charged, solar-charged, and AC- and solar-charged

As d.light's operations in Shenzhen expanded, they needed help from someone with more manufacturing experience. In late 2007, a mutual friend introduced Xian to a woman named SuShien Pang, who had been a manufacturing consultant in Shenzhen for several years. Su was looking for a new job, and when she sat down with Xian, and then Ned, she was intrigued. Ned invited her to come on board as d.light's first director of operations.

Before committing to the job, Su asked to travel to India to better understand the vision of d.light. Soon after meeting Sam and Erica in New Delhi, Su was pulled into a massive product rework of 3,000 problematic Novas. The capacitor on the circuit wasn't the right size, and all the products were at risk of overheating. It would only be the first of many reworks the d.light team had to undergo on its first product line.

"We had a bunch of daily workers," Su remembers. "We kept needing more workers. We had to check each day to see who could read, to see who could operate the multimeter." The conditions in their makeshift factory, which usually operated as a call center, were less than ideal. Su recalls seeing rat feces on the tables; her camera was stolen at one point. "They were totally bootstrapping it," she says of the d.light team. "They had no idea what was going on."

Despite these obvious challenges, Su was impressed by the high impact of d.light's products. In one home in India, she visited a family that had multiple daughters. Su asked if she could hold the youngest daughter, a baby. The mother spoke as she handed the baby to Su.

"She says you can take the baby, as long as you educate her," Su's friend and interpreter, Aarthi Jambhulka, who would later join d.light in India, told her.

Su had previously spent a significant amount of time in emerging markets, including China and Guatemala, but this really stuck with her. "They were so poor," Su explains. "They had all these daughters, and they would rather give one away so she could have a better life." These same families told her how much a prototype Nova had helped them, how it was a huge improvement over the kerosene they previously used.

After officially joining d.light, Su began assisting Ned, Xian, and Gabe in building the earliest d.light team in Shenzhen. They hired an administrative assistant named Amanda Liu, whose first day of work was at the apartment they had nearly burned down. "It was very strange," Amanda recalls. "They didn't even have an office. My interview was in a Starbucks. I went to work in an apartment." But Amanda was interested in a different kind of experience than the typical large corporation, and the mission and vision of d.light inspired her. The next hire was a sourcing manager named Stephen Deng, followed soon after by a couple engineers and quality control staff.

With Amanda's assistance, the team eventually secured a small 100-square-meter office on the twenty-second floor of an office high-rise in LuoHu. To save money, they purchased used office equipment that worked only some of the time. The air conditioner, a necessity in the hot and humid climate of Shenzhen, never seemed to get properly repaired. Amanda and Gabe bought supplies from the cheapest wholesale electronics market in Shenzhen and set up all the office internet wiring themselves.

The first d.light China office wasn't pretty, but it was enough to allow the team to set their sights on launching d.light's initial line of products.

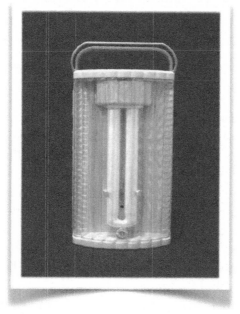

The Vega was similar to other CFL tube lights already available in the market

Chapter 9

DECISIONS AND TRANSITIONS

B y the end of 2007, the founders were faced with a serious dilemma. As high-volume manufacturing began in Shenzhen, and sales and marketing operations ramped up in New Delhi, it was becoming increasingly difficult to manage the work remotely. Everyone on the team traveled frequently, spending at least half their time in China or India, but they still struggled to collaborate effectively with partners on the ground.

Sam and Ned began having private conversations about how to resolve these challenges, and they kept coming back to the same solution: all of d.light's managers needed to relocate to China or India. A few of their investors and board members were in the U.S., but all their other collaborators were elsewhere. The company could only scale if its key people were in the markets where all the action was happening.

The decision wasn't easy to make, especially since they knew the implications were far-reaching. Ned and Gabe were both married; Sam and Erica were in serious dating relationships. Xian had wanted to apply for a green card and settle permanently in the U.S., but he would have to give up that dream if he moved to another country.

On a Thursday in November 2007, the five co-founders gathered for what they called "noodles." It was a weekly team dinner that was an open forum for the group. They were free to air concerns, address conflicts, or raise questions with one another. The original intent had been to have the conversation over take-out ramen noodles, which is why the meeting was called "noodles." "I don't think we ever actually had ramen together," Erica remembers, laughing. The food of choice tended to be burritos or Chinese food.

That's when Sam and Ned told the rest of the team their decision to move all the company's operations overseas. They asked Gabe and Xian to consider moving to China to oversee product design, engineering, and manufacturing, while Erica could move to India to lead customer research. Each co-founder was given a few months to make a decision. "It was a bit of a shock," Xian recalls. "But the rationale was sound."

Gabe understood right away that this was the solution to their many product-related challenges. "Not having people in China was

Gabe and Ned at a restaurant near the d.light office in Shenzhen in 2008

killing us," he says. "We had communication problems, time delays, lack of insights—all because we didn't have someone on the ground."

Gabe and his wife, Diana, seriously discussed moving to China. For a while, it looked like Diana might be given a big environmental consulting project in Shenzhen. But the project never came to fruition. In the end, they decided not to go. "Living in Shenzhen was too difficult," explains Gabe. "We wanted to have kids. Personally, being in China while starting a family wasn't something we wanted to take on." Gabe agreed to continue working for d.light, but it was mutually understood that this was not a long-term solution, and his decision not to move was the beginning of his transition out of the company.

Erica also agreed with the decision but was personally conflicted about what to do. "I always was of the belief that you have to be close to the people you are designing for," she explains. "I knew it was the best thing. But could I personally make it happen?" In addition, Erica had seen the toll that her father's frequent overseas stays had had on her mother and their family; she didn't want to do the same thing to her soon-to-be husband, Will.

When Erica was accepted for a fellowship at the Stanford Design School in the spring of 2008, she decided it was time to move on from d.light.

Xian, while also conflicted—especially about giving up his dream to live in the United States long term—agreed to move to Shenzhen in early 2008. Despite what he was sacrificing, he felt this was where he was called to go.

But life wasn't going to make it easy for him. In October 2007, Xian had torn the anterior cruciate ligament (ACL) in his left leg while playing basketball. It took seven weeks before he could be scheduled for surgery. In January 2008, only four weeks after the operation, he said good-bye to the United States and moved to China. He had been relying on crutches to get around for almost three months, but he was determined to begin life in China without crutches. Xian remembers being in significant pain the first week he was there, but he persevered as he began focusing on overseeing the work of the contract manufacturers.

Sam, of course, had known he would move to India the moment he and Ned made the decision to relocate the company's operations

Vanuatu: Light for an Underserved Island Nation

In 2009, a distribution partner on the South Pacific island nation of Vanuatu began ordering Novas and Solatas—and he kept ordering until he had enough units to provide light for 15 percent of the national population of 215,000.

In early 2010, Ned traveled to Vanuatu to understand the high demand there. He found an isolated country that is almost completely off-grid, with minimal access to imported products. Kerosene costs can be up at US$15 a month for a household.

Ned traveled with the distributor to the island of Tanna, which had not yet seen any d.light products. As they drove around, they were frequently stopped by customers who appeared out of the dense tropical foliage. Many pulled cash out of their pockets to purchase a Nova Mobile after just a few minutes of deliberation. Others said they would return later with money, and still others connected with local micro-finance organizations to finance the product.

In this extremely underserved market, the people had money but few good products to spend it on. The residents of Vanuatu also understand better than most the benefits of a solar-powered light for themselves and the environment. "It's good for climate change," a number of them told Ned.

By 2011, about 35 percent of households in Vanuatu owned a d.light product.

overseas. He had lived in India during his high school years, and he was leading the company's sales and marketing efforts. But the transition was still challenging.

He moved to India around the same time that Xian relocated to China, bringing only two suitcases with him. It was the middle of winter in New Delhi, when temperatures can dip to as low as 8 degrees centigrade (46 degrees Fahrenheit). The d.light team was being exceptionally frugal at the time, so Sam booked a room at a hotel with no heat and no hot water. Sam recalls, "It was freezing. I didn't know anyone. I didn't have any money."

Eventually he reconnected with a former biology teacher from his old high school. He invited Sam to sleep on a mattress in his home office for a while. Shortly after, Sam met an American couple —she worked for the United Nations and he was in information technology—who allowed Sam to stay in their extra room. With the help of Erica, who was still traveling to India to assist, he turned his attention to building a team in India.

Ned and his wife, Dorcas, were the last to move, relocating to Shenzhen in June 2008. Even though Ned had rented an apartment in a nice neighborhood in Shenzhen, their life in China didn't begin easily either. After about twenty-four hours of travel, they arrived at their apartment after midnight and found the entire place

Ned leads a team meeting in the first d.light China office

infested with cockroaches. "We didn't have any bug spray, and the stores were all closed," Ned recalls. "The only thing we could do was kill them ourselves." The exhausted couple stayed up until 3 a.m., smashing cockroaches with their shoes.

They officially joined the fledgling d.light China team the next day, with Ned managing the office and Dorcas taking on human resources and global communications. The Shenzhen team had about seven employees then but would soon begin to grow rapidly, adding more engineering, quality assurance, and logistics professionals.

When Ned first began overseeing Chinese Nationals on his team, he quickly learned that he needed to be very clear about his directives. He once asked Stephen, the sourcing manager, to make a list of potential suppliers for d.light. A couple days later, Stephen presented a spreadsheet of more than two hundred suppliers in Shenzhen. In the past forty-eight hours, he had barely slept, working at all hours to call every single one of them and record his findings in the spreadsheet.

"I was amazed at what Stephen had done," Ned remembers. "But I was also shocked. This was way more than what I had expected, and I felt really bad that he had spent so much time on it." Ned hadn't asked Stephen to come up with such an extensive list of suppliers or to contact each of them. At the same time, he realized, he hadn't asked Stephen *not* to do that. Ned promised his Chinese staff that, in the future, he would be much more detailed about his expectations.

Shortly thereafter, both offices began benefitting from an early initiative called the Fellows Program. The program recruited recent university graduates and young professionals who wanted hands-on experience in a growing social enterprise and didn't need a large salary. With backgrounds in business development, product design, engineering, and marketing, fellows typically came from the U.S. or Europe and relocated to Shenzhen or New Delhi, with d.light providing housing and a living stipend. They would usually stay for a six- to twelve-month commitment. At the end of their fellowship, some of them became permanent employees while others moved on to different opportunities. At times, these fellows made up as much as one-third of the team and brought a welcome infusion of energy and enthusiasm.

But the fellows, like the founders, had limited experience to bring to the table. And it was this lack of knowledge and skill within d.light as a whole that would cause some serious challenges for the young company as it began to do the real work of manufacturing products and selling them to distributors.

Some of the earliest members of the d.light China team, focusing on sourcing, engineering, logistics, and business development

Chapter 10

LESSONS IN INDIA

The d.light team had been trying to drum up sales in India since late 2007, but none of them had any previous experience with sales and distribution in India. The reality was that they had no idea what they were doing.

"We didn't know what we didn't know," Sam admits. "It's laughable what we did. We had to go through some of those painful things to learn."

Before even finalizing the first product line, Sam and Ned had met with various distributors in India to pitch a 500 rupee (about US$7) solar lantern. But they didn't yet know the final cost of manufacturing the product, nor had they taken into account all the costs that went into the value chain. None of the distributors was willing to take a chance on the new company and its unknown products—which turned out to be extremely fortunate. "If anyone had actually ordered, it would've bankrupted the company," Sam explains.

What d.light really needed was seasoned people with legitimate experience selling and distributing in India. After moving to India, Sam's first priority was hiring a head of sales. He tried to meet as many people as he could, taking advantage of any connection he could make. To save money, he traveled to these meetings in auto

Erica, who continued traveling to India several months after Sam moved, stands with the first container shipment of products from China to the India office

rickshaws through Delhi's notorious traffic. "I would work the whole way while I was in the auto rickshaw. My computer keys were always covered in pollution," Sam remembers. "It was such an inefficient and terrible process."

At the same time, he was trying to find an appropriate office space. Being a foreigner from a small, unknown company with few resources made it difficult for him to make any headway.

That's when Sam decided to recruit Aarthi Jambhulka, whom he had met when she acted as SuShien's interpreter during her field visit in India. Even though Aarthi had been born and raised in Pune, in the western Indian state of Maharashtra, she had never been exposed to rural life in her native country. In fact, when Su first told her about d.light, Aarthi didn't even believe there were people in India without access to electricity.

"SuShien told me she had met some people who were going to India to replace the kerosene lantern," she remembers. "I laughed and said, 'There are no kerosene lanterns in India. I don't know what these people are about.'" In fact, as many as 375 million people in India were off-grid at that time, nearly 30 percent of the global off-grid population. Almost all of them were using kerosene for lighting.[10] Hundreds of millions of other Indians had only intermittent electricity, so they also relied on kerosene or generators for light.

Aarthi began to learn this reality on the first trip she took out to rural villages in Uttar Pradesh. She remembers going with Su and Erica into various villages where it was common for people to carry homemade guns. For their own safety, the women had to make sure they returned to their hotel before it got dark outside.

But what struck Aarthi the most was the fact that kerosene was used everywhere in rural India. In the poorest areas of northern India, most families couldn't even afford a lantern, instead filling small medicine bottles with kerosene and using torn-up bits of cloth for wicks. "For me, it was really shocking to see they actually used kerosene lanterns. I didn't know people in my own country were in this situation," she explains. "I started to appreciate what d.light was doing."

When Sam contacted her about working for d.light, he was honest that he hadn't had any luck in recruiting other team members. Candidates would always ask him who else d.light was employing in India, and when he admitted that he hadn't hired anyone yet, they would elect to stay at their current jobs.

For Aarthi, however, it was an easy decision. "I saw the commitment of the founding team. They really wanted to make this difference, and they wanted to start in India," she says. She wasn't in a position where she needed financial support, so it was fine for her to join a risky start-up. She began work in February 2008 as the first official d.light India employee and the senior manager of special projects. "This means you have to do everything," Aarthi laughs. She began assisting Sam in multiple areas, including registering a d.light entity in India, opening bank accounts, and securing import licenses—which they only realized they needed after a container was already on its way from the Shenzhen office.

When registering an entity in India, they were asked to submit five different options for company names, in case some were already taken. Sam and Ned brainstormed multiple variations of d.light—d.light design, d.light lighting, d.light energy—and then ran out of ideas. They encountered the Hindi word *jadoo*, meaning *magic,* and, for fun, decided to add that as their final option: Jadoo Lighting.

A few weeks later, when Sam received notice of their official registration as an Indian company, he was shocked to find that they had been given the name Jadoo Lighting. Whoever had processed their registration must have liked that name best. For branding purposes, though, it was terrible. In the end, it took over a year to rectify the mistake and get the entity name changed to d.light Energy Private Limited.

Fortunately, the founders got it right when it came to other important matters. Aarthi remembers encountering a few corrupt officials who demanded bribes in exchange for sales licenses. When she asked Sam how to respond, he was very clear with her. "It doesn't matter if our company doesn't go forward," he told her. "Don't bend on any bribes, Aarthi. It will be okay." And it was. When the officials saw that the d.light team refused to pay any bribes, they eventually released their licenses.

A couple of months after Aarthi joined, Sam met someone who was finishing construction on an office building in Noida, a suburb of Delhi. He offered d.light the use of a small office on the third

Bihar, India: Products that Don't Fail

As the head of customer experience in India, Pankaj Arora frequently travels to the market to meet with d.light customers. During one such trip to the state of Bihar, he met a woman who owned an S300. She told him she had  purchased the product four years prior, and was still using it.

"In front of me, she was telling people around that this is the product which they should buy because it doesn't fail," Pankaj recalls. "I was happy to know that our products are so reliable. That gave me a thrill."

floor in exchange for a reasonable rent. "We had two little rooms in an unoccupied, massive office building," Sam recalls. He and Aarthi officially opened the d.light India office on June 1, 2008.

Several new hires started work a few days later: Rajendra Gupta, head of sales; Ravindra Kumar, head of business development, and Kiran Gaikwad, a young product designer fresh out of university. They were joined soon after by three fellows from Stanford: recent MBA graduates Jeremy Utley and Frederico Lozano, and engineering graduate Joe Mellin.

The mixed origins of the team led, unsurprisingly, to many cross-cultural misunderstandings. In one staff meeting, Jeremy reported positively on staff morale, based on one-on-one meetings he had conducted. Immediately after, Rajendra began to talk about their cash status, stating that the office had "seven lakhs," or 700,000 rupees, in the bank.

Most of the foreigners in the room weren't familiar with the term. Turning to Rajendra, Jeremy demanded to know why he hadn't shared these "lacks," or shortcomings, during their one-on-

The earliest members of the d.light India team, focusing on product design, sales, business development, marketing, and distribution

one meeting. Rajendra, in turn, could not fathom why Jeremy was suddenly so upset. Only Sam and Aarthi understood the miscommunication, laughing about it even as they did their best to explain to the rest of the team.

As Sam and Ned had expected, India turned out to be an extremely tough market to start in. And their earlier decision to work with a low-quality manufacturer in Shenzhen was coming back to haunt them. When units of the Comet and Vega arrived in India in the summer of 2008, they were in terrible shape. The bendable gooseneck of the Comet would easily pop out of the product. The Vega circuit boards were so badly soldered that components would regularly fall off. "It was a disaster," Ned remembers. "The products were so bad that we couldn't sell them under our brand." They knew the reputation of d.light had to be based on quality; these products did not pass the test.

"The quality control was very bad," Xian explains. "We were learning the pros and cons of controlling the process ourselves versus letting the contract manufacturers do it all." The team had learned a painful, costly lesson that quality couldn't be sacrificed for price, and quality had to begin with the quality of the manufacturing partners.

Within weeks, the team went from preparing for the launch of an entire product line to introducing a single product into the market: the Nova. Customers in India responded well to the Nova, with its unique form factor and high-quality production. "I still believe that it was the best product of its kind available at the time," Ned says. "Even today, we still find customers using those original Novas." But customers also complained that the cost, at more than US$30, was too high. The Nova Mobile, which offered mobile phone charging and could also be AC-charged, was released a few months later. It cost even more.

Along the way, plenty of other problems arose. The d.light team in India had to learn about compliance and importing, primarily through mistakes. And product issues continued to plague them.

Once an entire container of Novas arrived in Delhi from the Shenzhen office—only to be dropped while being moved from the container ship. Every light in the container short-circuited; not a single one would turn on. But these lights had already been sold, and distributors were demanding to know where their units were.

There were no engineers in the India office. SuShien immediately flew out from China to oversee the effort to rework the units, soldering the circuit boards and replacing the batteries. Team members trained in business and sales and marketing pitched in, beginning work at 5:30 a.m. day after day until all the units were repaired.

Despite all the challenges, there were moments when the young India team knew that they were on to something. Once, after hearing from a discouraged sales team that the products were too expensive and solar was too new of a technology, Sam, Aarthi, and Joe took a spontaneous sales trip to a village to demonstrate demand for the products. They made a brief sales presentation about d.light and the Nova, and the villagers came in droves to purchase units.

Another time, they brought a prospective partner into the field to see their sales team in action. So many customers wanted to buy a d.light lantern that, as the sun was setting, they tried to stop the team from returning to Delhi. Even after the d.light employees got into the car, "people were throwing money through the window, begging for products," Aarthi recalls.

These experiences taught Sam and his colleagues a valuable lesson: Customers in India wanted the products and many had the money to purchase them. d.light just needed to do a better job of reaching them.

Chapter 11

THE CONTAINER MIRACLE

While the focus of sales was definitely India, the d.light team occasionally received inquiries from other countries. They had received excellent press coverage in the U.S. after winning the DFJ competition and raising seed funding, including features in *Fortune* magazine and *Fast Company*, and mentions in periodicals like *TIME* and *The New York Times*.

The sales inquiries would come directly to Ned and Sam, or through the d.light website. Intern Angela Cheung, a Haas School of Business graduate, was tasked with managing any online inquiries. Aside from that, d.light didn't have any sales strategy for geographies outside of India.

Back in January 2008, a woman with a U.S.-based NGO that wanted to provide solar power in Tanzania visited the d.light office in Mountain View to purchase some samples. She liked the Nova so much that she decided to place an order of 5,400 units, at a cost of nearly US$90,000, in the spring of 2008.

It was the largest order d.light had ever received, and the first container they would be shipping outside of India. The operations team worked long hours to get the container of products out on time, and the China team had a small celebration the day the container officially left port and began its journey to East Africa.

*Small shipments of the Nova arrive at the Shenzhen office
to meet orders from outside India*

The celebration didn't last long, though. A couple weeks later, the China team realized that a serious error had been made in the engineering of the product. "The code on the micro-controller had a one-line bug," Gabe recalls. "It was my fault. There was a last-minute change to the characteristics of the light. I made the change but didn't catch the error. So the units never went to low-power sleep."

Without ever fully going to sleep, the Novas were actively draining their batteries as they sat on the container ship. By the time the units arrived in Tanzania, the deep discharge would have permanently killed the batteries. The lights would never even turn on.

The first container order d.light ever got, initially a cause for great celebration, could now destroy the entire company.

Ned notified the team in India, which was also receiving a container of the defective products. They began planning for yet another major product rework, one of at least three that they had to do in 2008. Su flew out to India once again to assist. It would cost the company US$30,000 to fix all the units in India.

As for the container that was on its way to Tanzania, there were limited options. The units had to be recoded and all the batteries replaced. Ned and Su began discussing what it would require to set up a team in Africa to fix the units. They considered sending out a new container with working products—but it would take weeks to manufacture enough to fulfill the order.

On top of that, Sam and Ned were actively speaking with d.light's existing investors about a Series A investment round. The company had enough cash to last through the end of 2008, but they would need more funding if they wanted to continue to scale. Nexus had already expressed interest in leading the round. But if the d.light team could not rectify this product challenge, all the funding could be in jeopardy.

An air of desperation settled over the China office as team members worked day and night, battling frustration and anxiety in hopes of finding a solution.

In the end, a clerical error saved the company. d.light didn't yet have the capacity to manage multinational logistics, so the NGO had engaged a third-party logistics company to manage the shipment of the container from Shenzhen to Dar es Salaam, Tanzania. The logistics company needed a bill of lading from the NGO but never told them. As a result, the container of Novas had been detained at a port in Oman, in the Middle East, for several weeks. In the desert heat, the interior of containers can reach more than 50 degrees centigrade (or 122 degrees Fahrenheit), enough to damage even the most robust electronics. Even if the Novas had

Some of the first Novas to come off the mass production line

been programmed perfectly, they would not have been functioning by the time they arrived in Tanzania.

The NGO customer was deeply frustrated about the delay, but most of that was directed toward the logistics company. Ned patiently explained how the heat could adversely affect the products and offered to send the container back to China to have the units reworked. The customer expressed their appreciation for d.light's customer service, none the wiser about the original defect in the product. The disaster had been averted. "It was a miracle," Xian remembers.

Another disaster loomed, though, one that d.light had nothing to do with. The global economy was beginning to show serious signs of trouble in the fall of 2008. Major institutions in the U.S., such as Lehman Brothers, AIG, and Washington Mutual Bank, were collapsing as stock markets around the world crashed. Investors in every region were beginning to hold on to their money, unwilling to take any risks in the volatile economy.

While fears of a global recession built, the original investors in d.light decided to keep their commitments to put in more money for a Series A round. Nexus led the round with US$2.5 million, while Acumen added another US$800,000 and Gray Matters US$750,000. Mahindra, Garage, and DFJ also contributed, leading to a total of US$4.9 million. Unlike the last round, this one wasn't a convertible note but a typical purchase for shares.

On the day all the investors signed the final agreement, Ned anxiously watched the international news from his base in Shenzhen. It was October 2, 2008. Just three days earlier, the US Congress had rejected a large government bailout package that would have rescued many of the failing financial institutions.[11] It was unclear if they would change their minds. Global stock markets continued to nosedive, and many investors were panicking.

"I was sitting at my computer, and I kept refreshing the page for our bank account," Ned recalls. He was waiting anxiously for the funding to come through, hoping that the investors wouldn't pull the plug at the last minute because of the impending financial crisis. They had agreed to wire the funds to d.light within twenty-four hours of signing the agreement. "I must have hit refresh a hundred times in less than one hour."

At long last, the balance of the company's bank account jumped up. And jumped up again. And again. Every investor had kept their word. d.light had enough financial runway to keep going for another year. The next day, the American Congress approved a US$700 billion bailout package that was the first step toward stabilizing global markets.

Later that same month, the China team reshipped a container of Novas—now functioning—to East Africa. It had taken two months to bring the container back to Shenzhen and have all the units repaired. The India team had also managed to repair their units and could begin selling in earnest.

It had been a harrowing few months for d.light, but somehow, against all odds, the company had lived to see another day.

Tanzania: Prioritizing Education for the Next Generation

When the Tanzania team organized their first road show to market the Solata, business development manager Angela Cheung and her colleagues traveled through the areas around the city of Arusha.

After one of the sales presentations, a large number of women purchased Solatas. Angela asked a colleague to survey them to find out why people were buying the lights. Most customers said the light was for their children to study and be able to remain in school.

"It was really neat to see women, many of them without an education themselves, be able to use their money to support their children's education," Angela explains.

Chapter 12

WHAT DIDN'T WORK

From its founding, one of d.light's strongest competitive advantages was its empathic, human-centered approach to product design, honed by the founders' experience at the Stanford Design School. Even as the team struggled to make a high-quality solar lantern at a low price point, they remained hopeful that, with the right people, this was possible. They hired British national Robin Chilton, who had significant experience as a product design consultant, as the company's first head of product design.

Robin moved to New Delhi in November 2008 as the thirteenth employee of the team there. His first impression of d.light? "It was pretty chaotic," he remembers. "Everything was always changing, even from my interview to when I started. What was on the agenda was not what we actually did."

His first priorities were to put some procedures and structures in place in what had been a fairly ad hoc product development process. He worked with Sam, Ned, Xian, and others to begin to establish a product roadmap.

But, for everyone involved, there was a lot to learn. "My approach was to make a lot of mistakes," Robin admits with a laugh. "I would fail quickly." It didn't take long for Robin to realize just how much he didn't know. His previous projects had all been for European and American consumers. Unsurprisingly, he brought strong Western sensibilities about functionality and aesthetics into his approach.

This was quickly challenged by his colleague Kiran Gaikwad, whose proposed designs—dismissed by the expatriates in the office —were consistently far more well-liked by Indian consumers than anything Robin came up with. "I had to humble myself and realize that there was a lot I didn't know," Robin reflects. The vast distinctions in culture and values between people from different countries, he realized, could not be underestimated.

Similarly, his first experience designing for base-of-the-pyramid customers led to some eye-opening insights. "My initial thought was just about making the products cheap, but actually, our customers wanted things that were very high value. They had to be very durable," Robin explains. "If they're going to put this money down, that's a big investment for them. They have to have confidence that it's going to work." His mindset shifted to recognizing that d.light products were often "the most expensive thing they've spent their money on."

By this time, the d.light team had permanently moved away from AC-charged products and decided to focus exclusively on

Members of the product design team meet with rural households in India to learn about their energy needs

solar. The cost of solar photovoltaic technology had been dropping steadily, making the small solar panels that d.light used increasingly affordable. All trends pointed toward even further cost reductions in the future. They also found that more and more countries, including India, were waiving import duties for solar products. Anything AC-charged would still be taxed, leading to far higher prices for the end consumer.

The decision to pursue solar also made sense from an engineering standpoint. The wild fluctuations in voltages of the electricity that flowed through the grid or generators in emerging markets were nearly impossible to manage with a small, low-cost circuit. The sun provided a far steadier source of energy.

From Robin's first day with d.light, he knew that one of his main goals would be designing a solar lamp that reached the elusive US$5 price point that the founding team had set its sights on. They nicknamed the project Spud, a reference to their hope that this product would be as low-cost and ubiquitous as potatoes.

Robin and his team reviewed the ethnographic research that had previously been done, but they needed more information. They spent months visiting villages in India, prototyping, testing, and then prototyping and testing some more. "It took a really long time," he remembers.

Along the way, the product design team had plenty of other projects to distract them. One of d.light's competitors had released a small solar panel that directly charged mobile phones, and it was doing really well in Africa. Robin was asked to come up with something similar. His team traveled to Nigeria for research and developed a small solar power pack for mobile phones. But they couldn't get the prototypes to work properly, and the project ultimately lost traction.

Then the Indian telecommunications company Airtel expressed interest in a similar phone charger that could be bundled with their lowest-cost mobile phones in India. Again, the product design team got to work on prototyping a solar phone charger, in hopes that this might be the big break d.light needed in India.

But the design team made an assumption about Indian consumers that significantly hurt the project. On-the-ground research had shown that households typically paid to have their phones charged once every three days. As a result, the d.light prototype had enough capacity to charge one-third of a phone battery. Robin and his team thought this was perfect: instead of paying for a full battery charge every three days, customers could use a much lower-cost solar panel to charge one-third of their battery each day.

Unfortunately, that defied the conventional thinking of rural Indians at the time, which was that phone batteries worked best when they were charged from empty to full. Consumers thought a product that only partially charged their phones would damage the batteries, and were reluctant to use the prototypes. On top of that, Airtel was demanding a price point that d.light simply couldn't meet. "The prices of batteries and solar panels hadn't fallen enough yet," Robin explains. The Airtel partnership never came to fruition.

While the d.light team continued to prioritize a low-cost solar lantern, interest in a solar home system dated back to as early as 2008. Back then, the push was for a minimal system—little more

Co-Creating with Customers

Robin Chilton's favorite customer stories involve consumers who took d.light products and found creative uses for them. "I remember there was one village in U.P. that we would visit often," he says. There they met a man who had purchased an S10. On the next visit, they found he had purchased another d.light lantern, and yet another one on the next visit. "Eventually he had seven or eight in his home. He wanted to become a salesperson for us," Robin remembers.

In East Africa, Robin and his team often encountered customers who wanted to use d.light products to start phone-charging businesses. He loved how entrepreneurial and creative they were. "They were essentially saying, 'I'm going to take your product, and I'm going to do something with it that will benefit me even more.' It was enabling other activities, allowing them to do more," Robin explains. "It was the concept of co-creation, stretched out over time. It was great to see what people had done with the products."

than a large panel with a large-capacity battery and wires that could plug into several devices—that would be affordable enough for customers to purchase in cash. "The top-end Nova that included mobile phone charging cost about 1,700 rupees at the time. Our aim was for a home system that cost 2,500 rupees," Robin explains. "What it could do at that price wasn't that much, but it could at least give the experience of a home system."

Ultimately the home system project, nicknamed Kit, didn't materialize into anything. Market research showed that customers wanted far more than what the d.light prototype could offer. But it wasn't possible to develop the home system customers wanted without raising the price significantly, far beyond what base-of-the-pyramid families could afford.

This challenge of affordability, and what possible solutions existed to address that, was becoming increasingly significant. Even from the first day of d.light's incorporation, on May 17, 2007, the team had considered the burgeoning micro-finance industry in South Asia, which provided very small loans to mostly women in organized accountability groups, as a key partnership opportunity. That day, Ned sent an email to an executive at SKS Microfinance, then one of the largest micro-finance institutions in India. He made an initial pitch to them but didn't hear back.

It wasn't until late 2008 that SKS was ready to experiment with a cross-sale business that would offer products to its millions of established customers. They agreed to do a pilot with d.light's Nova Mobile product with customers in the state of Odisha. SKS would make the solar lantern available to their customers, who could add the cost of the product to their existing loan. It was the first time d.light products would be financed.

Given the scale of SKS's business, even a pilot was no small matter. "We were running pilots in four districts of India with 13 branches," Sam recalls. For the still young company, it was a huge operation to provide thousands of Novas to the micro-finance institution.

The pilot was not without its complications. The deep discharge issue that had plagued the first container order to Africa also affected the units in the SKS pilot, so the units had to be reworked and repaired before being provided for customers. Later on, the team upgraded the batteries in the Nova from sealed-lead-acid

Product designers collect feedback from Indian customers about the Nova Mobile

batteries to much better performing nickel-metal-hydride (NiMH) batteries. But the new batteries were considerably lighter in weight —and customers noticed. Customers worried that the lighter weight meant reduced quality and performance, and they did not hesitate to complain to representatives from SKS. The d.light team in India had to deal with irate customers and frustrated SKS managers for weeks. They conducted many public drop tests of the Nova, including one from the top of the five-story building that the d.light office was in, to assure customers that the products were still extremely durable.

Despite these mishaps, their efforts paid off. Sam remembers how SKS managers told him that "these things are selling faster than anything else we've tested. People are using them like crazy." Over the course of four months, a total of 1,540 lights were sold through SKS branches. A follow-up study conducted by SKS found stunning results: 98 percent of SKS customers who purchased a Nova Mobile were highly satisfied with the product, while 88 percent reported at least one income-boosting benefit from the light and 80 percent said that it had become their most important source of light. End users reported using the lights for everything from delivering babies and studying to warding off dangerous herds of elephants.

In the wake of this unqualified success, the two companies began having serious conversations about expanding their partnership across the whole of India.

Then, in mid-2009, SKS made the abrupt decision to close down its cross-sale business. Only later did the d.light team understand that there were significant internal changes happening within SKS due to their upcoming initial public offering, the first of its kind in India.[12]

Back then, all they knew was that the prospect of a pan-India deal with SKS had suddenly evaporated. Despite their disappointment, Sam realizes now that it was for the best. "It would've taken us from 1,000 units a month to 30,000 units a month," he explains. "In hindsight, the deal not happening was one of the luckiest things. We wouldn't have been able to scale up that quickly."

But this success in India had given the leadership team a sense of what might be possible one day. In collaboration with an intern with expertise in branding, they began reworking the company's mission and vision statements.

d.light had started with the mission to eradicate kerosene—a worthy goal that was hard to measure and could take decades to reach. The founders realized that a more concrete, quantifiable target could better focus their efforts. So, around that time, they established a big, ambitious goal: to reach 100 million customers by 2020. This would mean that 10 percent of the current off-grid population would have switched from kerosene to solar power, which was no small feat in and of itself. "This would be a good start," Ned remembers thinking at the time. "It would make a significant dent in addressing the problem of kerosene."

They would get a big boost toward reaching this target with help from an entirely different part of the world.

Chapter 13

INTO AFRICA

One day in 2008, a distributor from Nigeria showed up in the Shenzhen office, unannounced, and asked to meet with Ned. The distributor, it turns out, was carrying a duffel bag full of tens of thousands of dollars in cash. He said he had heard about d.light from news reports and was ready to place a large order of Novas that day. Ned and his team were stunned, and scrambled to meet the distributor's request.

He wasn't the only one. Over time, more and more distributors from Africa contacted d.light through its website after hearing about the company through the media or word of mouth. Even though every d.light business plan had focused on Asia, and their initial sales and marketing efforts were all focused on India, it was becoming hard to ignore the demand coming out of Africa. Sam and Ned began to wonder about the possibility of expanding operations into sub-Saharan Africa.

In late 2008, they fortuitously met Pepijn Steemers, a Dutch businessman based in Tanzania. Through another organization, Pepijn had had great success in selling fourteen-watt solar home systems to middle-income households. The cost was a high US$200, but it was the only smaller-scale solar product available for Tanzanian households.

Then Pepijn heard how new portable solar lanterns were coming out. Realizing that this might be the key to making solar more accessible and affordable for Tanzanians, Pepijn asked his organization's board if he could start selling solar lights to lower-income customers. His board insisted that he stick with home systems.

Dismayed, but also certain that portable lanterns could open up the solar market in Tanzania, Pepijn left to start his own distribution business. He flew to Shenzhen to meet with another solar company for a distribution deal. That meeting didn't go well—and Sam and Ned, seeing an opportunity to partner with an experienced businessman in East Africa, intercepted him.

"We convinced him that d.light's going places," Sam recalls. They encouraged Pepijn not to be simply a distributor but to join d.light as a managing director, leading their sales and marketing efforts in Tanzania.

Pepijn was excited by the idea, but he had some clear conditions. He wanted to sell a solar-powered desk lamp, similar to what the competitor company he met with had. And he wanted huge volumes. d.light had to commit to producing close to 100,000 units before he was willing to come on board—a scale that they had never

Pepijn pilots a small plane, with Ned as passenger, to visit rural areas in Tanzania

manufactured at before. Never ones to shirk away from a challenge, Sam and Ned agreed.

Within a few days, the co-founders, Pepijn, and Pepijn's colleague Sjoerd Spaanjaars had struck a deal to open the first d.light Africa office in Dar es Salaam. "We agreed on how we wanted to do it," Pepijn recalls. "Then they wired us $150,000 to help start the company, and that's what we did."

Because of the high real estate costs in Dar es Salaam, Pepijn decided to rent a building that doubled as his home and the d.light Africa office. He and Sjoerd registered the company and hired their first sales manager, an experienced salesman from Unilever named Joseph Mutishopia. Angela Cheung temporarily moved from the Shenzhen office to assist with business development, and Laura Smaitz, a Dutchwoman, came in as a marketing intern.

At the same time, the product design and engineering staff developed schematics for the new desk lamp based on existing products. A Tanzanian marketing firm recommended the name *Solata*, a derivative of *solar light* in Kiswahili. The operations team in China worked with the contract manufacturer to produce an initial batch of 5,000 units, which were shipped over to Tanzania. In a test pilot, Pepijn and his small team sold all 5,000 units in only two days.

Thrilled at their success, Sam and Ned gave the go-ahead to produce another 93,000 Solatas. Completing this number in time would require manufacturing at least 3,000 a day. Their current contract manufacturers simply weren't able to produce such high volumes, and it would take far too long to increase their capacity.

Operations director Su decided to take the project to a watch factory that was managed by someone she knew. "We were stuck, and they could help us out in a pinch," Su explains. But it was no small feat to train the factory workers on an entirely new type of product. It took several months to get production of the Solatas up and running.

The small team in Tanzania began receiving products to sell in the fall of 2009. Their primary sales strategy, explains Pepijn, was to follow the fast-moving consumer goods (FMCG) route to market. They focused on road shows in rural areas, making their pitch directly to consumers or small shop owners.

Angela was tasked with overseeing the first d.light road show across rural Tanzania. The d.light team rented a large van, hired a team of about fifteen young dancers, and traveled to various marketplaces to make their pitch. "We would roll into a place, set up a tent, put up signs and banners, then set up speakers and turn up the music really loud. The dancers would start dancing, and this would draw a crowd," Angela remembers.

Once a group of onlookers gathered, an external marketing consultant pitched the Solata in Kiswahili. The dancers doubled as sales agents, bringing units into the crowd and collecting the payments of 20,000 Tanzanian shillings (about US$14.30) for each Solata.

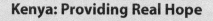

Kenya: Providing Real Hope

Alex Olum, general manager of Kenya, once visited a new D30 customer with several colleagues. The d.light employees were there to install and activate the home system.

When they arrived, it was about six in the evening. "As the light was fading, the kids were playing outside," recounts Alex. "We put on the lights for them to see. But one of the children started crying because he thought the house was on fire. He was crying and refused to go into the house because he had not seen that big of a light in his life."

Only after the mother intervened, carrying her child toward the house and showing him that it was safe, did he calm down and enter his home to enjoy the new lights.

Seeing this family's reaction to having light for the first time brought Alex to tears. "I knew that today I had given real hope by just selling to this home," he reflects.

The first road show team in Tanzania

"The road show was really fun, but it was also really tough," says Angela. Only the marketing consultant and one of the dancers spoke some English, and Angela didn't speak any Kiswahili. Without being able to communicate, it was challenging to manage the team. In addition, they were spending long hours under the hot sun day after day. On multiple occasions Angela became seriously ill with what was likely heatstroke.

On a typical day, the road show team sold about twenty to thirty Solatas in one location; if they encountered a shop owner who was willing to buy a box or two of 12 Solatas, then they would sell more. Angela estimates that they sold a few hundred Solatas in total. Compared to the expectations that Pepijn had set, these numbers were disappointing.

In the following months, the Tanzania team kept doing road shows—as many as eight simultaneously—across the country. But customers still weren't buying. "My anticipation of the light was that it would just fly," Pepijn recalls. "The lights started pouring in from China, but the sales weren't picking up."

Why the team was unable to replicate their initial success remains a mystery, but the experience provided a valuable lesson for d.light. "A similar thing has happened to us multiple times," Sam reflects. "Sometimes you just have an incredible one-off hit.

But it's important to stress test things in a few areas before making really big decisions." Making assumptions based on one highly encouraging data point can be risky and costly.

One of the most significant challenges, Pepijn believes, was that the idea of a portable solar lantern was an entirely new category for Tanzanian customers in 2009. They needed to understand the product better, to be convinced that it was worth the risk to spend the relatively large sum of US$14.30. The few families who had previously encountered solar had mostly had terrible experiences, having been sold poor quality or even fake solar products in the past. They needed to be persuaded that d.light products were different.

"This is one of the most risk-averse, skeptical customer populations in the world," Ned explains. "In the beginning, most of them didn't know about solar. They didn't know our brand. There was no reason for them to trust us." Despite the quality of the products and the significant benefits they offered to consumers, the lights weren't going to sell themselves. Customers had to be convinced it was a worthy investment of their hard-earned cash.

In later road shows, the Tanzania team made adjustments accordingly. They learned to rely less on entertainment and more on detailed sales pitches. Pepijn explains why this was significant. "You could have someone come one day, listen to the explanation, buy the product, and then they would come back the next day to buy another one, but they wanted to hear the explanation all over again," he recalls. Educating consumers was an effective approach, but it was incredibly time- and resource-consuming.

Meanwhile, Pepijn still had more than 60,000 Solatas filling almost every room of his home and office—which led to other problems. After about six months of being unused, the Solata batteries would begin to suffer damage unless they were recharged. The Africa team brought on technicians to recharge all the batteries. They ended up staying on to fix a container of faulty Novas. Su flew from Shenzhen to train the technicians on how to rework the printed circuit boards (PCBs) and replace the batteries on 40,000 Novas. Team members also went to Malawi and Mozambique to rework defective Novas that had been sold there.

The Tanzanian team had to divert significant resources to such ongoing repair and maintenance efforts, even as they struggled to expand sales. "We had four technicians employed full-time for this, and they were constantly busy for at least a year and a half," explains Pepijn.

By mid-2010, about a year after the first Solatas had arrived, the growing desperation of the Tanzanian team pushed them to employ a scattershot strategy that Pepijn now admits was deeply flawed. "We did twenty things at the same time out of despair of not selling lights," he remembers. "This was not sensible. We couldn't do this properly. Not enough matters got enough attention."

The d.light team's bullish, aggressive approach to Tanzania was proving to be extremely costly. They had underestimated how much time and effort was required to seed the market and win customers over to a new and risky value proposition. As the Tanzania office continued to operate in the red, they were increasingly in need of something to break open. But it wasn't clear where that would come from.

Ned, Su, and others from the China team partner with factory employees on a rework of Solatas

Chapter 14

THE KEROSENE KILLER

On top of the issues in Tanzania, d.light was facing a significant shortage of funding. When the pan-India deal with SKS Microfinance fell through in 2009, it sank an even more critical deal. A top venture capital firm in Silicon Valley, which also happened to be an investor in SKS, had wanted to lead d.light's Series B fundraising round. They conducted their due diligence and even went so far as to send a term sheet offering US$5 million in equity.

But when SKS shut down its cross-sale business, and d.light no longer seemed on the trajectory for exponential growth, the investor lost interest. They walked away, leaving the company in an increasingly precarious financial situation. "We had planned out our cash with the expectation that we would have received funding by December 2009," Ned remembers. "When that investor fell through, we were in trouble."

Sam and Ned immediately began looking for other investors, but the process inevitably took a long time. Investment firms were slow to respond. They had many requests and questions. They wanted to visit the regional offices and meet customers as part of their due diligence. In the meantime, d.light came ever closer to running out of money.

The co-founders had been down this road before, but now, with nearly fifty employees across three offices, a monthly production rate around 10,000 units, and an existing customer base of about 200,000, the stakes were far higher. It wasn't just about keeping the dream of d.light alive. They wanted their employees to retain their jobs; they hoped to maintain good relationships with their growing network of suppliers and distributors; and they were determined to provide after-sales services and even better products for their growing customer base.

The two leaders did whatever they could to creatively stretch d.light's cash reserves as long as possible, including working without pay for several months. "It was so stressful," Sam explains. "We kept looking for funding, but we didn't know where it was going to come from or when it was going to come."

In the meantime, there was still plenty of work to keep the team busy. On October 21, 2009, d.light officially released its third major product after the Nova and the Solata: the Kiran, which means *beam* or *ray of light* in Hindi.

Building Empathy for Customers

For years, all d.light executives participated in quarterly empathy trips that involved personally connecting with customers in the field. The hope was that no one in the organization, no matter their role, would lose touch with the needs and wants of d.light customers.

David Small, the first managing director in Kenya, remembers going to a Kenyan village and meeting a woman who had purchased an S10. "She prostrated herself on the ground in front of me to thank me for the difference this light had made in her life," he recalls. "I never forgot that. Seeing that impact, hearing it directly from her, that's what kept me going through tough times."

Getting a new product out hadn't been easy. With the design processes still being formulated, the many iterations of prototyping and field testing that the nascent product team underwent resulted in a process that took about fifteen months.

This was the first d.light product that had been developed especially for the Indian consumer, with every part of its shape and functionality informed by interviews with off-grid families in India. Based on the product roadmap that had been created when Robin first joined, the Kiran was positioned as a direct competitor to the kerosene lantern. The d.light team dubbed it "the kerosene killer." Even the form factor intentionally resembled a lantern so it would seem familiar to consumers—with one key and very intentional difference.

During one of their field visits, a villager made a comment to the design team that really stuck with them. "He said, 'Every lantern has a dark shadow underneath it,'" Robin remembers. "It meant that every person who is giving out light has something dark and sinister underneath them." It also, very practically, referred to the

These two children in India became some of the main faces of the Kiran marketing campaign

metal base of a kerosene lantern, which did indeed create a dark shadow within the circle of light that it cast.

The Kiran, as a result, was intentionally designed with a translucent base so it wouldn't cast a dark shadow. Customers really loved the design, which also sent an important message about d.light. "The brand of d.light is transparent," Robin explains. "We're a shining light. We're not trying to exploit people. There is no shadow."

Everything about the Kiran, from its name to its bright blue color, had been designed according to Indian consumer preferences. It was also the first d.light product to incorporate the solar panel into the product itself, thanks to newly developed heat-resistant nickel-metal-hydride batteries and a careful industrial design that allowed for sufficient heat ventilation. The Kiran's US$12 price point was the lowest for a portable solar lantern in the industry.

But it was still too expensive. The Kiran was not able to live up to its internal nickname, Spud. The final price point was way above that of potatoes, and far from the wished-for US$5. It was also far too expensive for a consumer population that had easy access to government-subsidized kerosene.[13]

The main hindrance to reducing costs, explains Robin, was that the design team and operations team weren't talking to one another. Product design was based in New Delhi, while manufacturing was in Shenzhen. In addition, members of the design team were all Indian or British, and the engineers were all Chinese. Without close collaboration between the two functions, the design team was designing without any knowledge of how their decisions would impact manufacturing processes and costs.

About six to nine months into the design process for the Kiran, Robin and his team finally traveled to Shenzhen to meet with their engineering colleagues and visit the factories. Even then, the two sides could never quite get on the same page, and as a result, the design couldn't be optimized for base-of-the-pyramid customers.

It's a lesson that Robin now frequently passes on to other aspiring product designers. "Get out there and understand how things are actually made. You will fail at design if you don't know how things are made," he says. Only after he began interacting closely with engineers and contract manufacturers did Robin understand that the most minute design decisions, such as how many bends went into a wire, had significant ramifications on the final cost of the product.

Despite these challenges, the d.light team still hoped that the Kiran would catalyze explosive sales in India. The product got great international media coverage and garnered several international design awards, including the highest design award from Spark and the best-designed consumer product award from Design Week.

Even then, the Kiran didn't move at the volumes the team had hoped for. They were coming to learn a hard truth: even if they designed the highest quality, most affordable product, it couldn't succeed without effective marketing and distribution strategies. In a world of push products and pull products, solar lanterns were undoubtedly push products. And the d.light team was just beginning to grasp how much push would be required for customers to take a chance on one of their products.

In response to these challenges, Sam and Ned made two major strategic shifts. They decided to relocate the entire product design team to Hong Kong, bringing Robin and his colleagues in much closer proximity with the manufacturing operations. They also knew they needed far more experienced sales executives in India and Africa, who understood the ins and outs of their respective markets in a way that Sam and Ned couldn't.

Soon after the Kiran was released, Sam handed over leadership of the India office to new managing director Mandeep Singh, who had previously overseen rural sales and distribution for multinational corporation Kodak. Sam then moved to Hong Kong to support the product design team and Africa team. Ned would join him in Hong Kong shortly afterwards, turning the new Hong Kong office into an important center of decision-making for d.light.

In Africa, the co-founders began looking for a more experienced managing director to lead d.light's Africa operations, perhaps based in another country. They had established an office in Dar es Salaam primarily because of Pepijn and his previous experience and success, but they weren't sure that was the most strategic location for pan-Africa work.

It was just the beginning of a huge season of change for d.light, full of experimentation, learning, and new directions. One of those major new opportunities came in the form of an email that almost got lost.

Children in Micronesia with the Kiran

Chapter 15

In the fall of 2009, global energy provider Total Energy sent an email to d.light and its competitors. Total was launching a new initiative to sell solar lamps in their many petrol stations in Africa. They wanted to run two different pilots, one in Cameroon and one in Senegal, and were seeking potential suppliers to present proposals to them in Paris.

The email went to one of d.light's business development fellows. He read the email and assumed that pursuing this would be a waste of time. Little d.light working with a giant like Total? It was too hard to believe. The fellow deleted the email without telling anyone about the request for proposal. When someone from Total called to follow up, the fellow told him that d.light wouldn't be participating.

Then, someone from Total sent another email on October 21, 2009—this time directly to Ned, who was visiting the India office at the time. When he read the email, Ned saw an incredible opportunity, one that d.light had almost missed. Total was asking potential suppliers to travel to Paris to meet with them in person during the week of October 26-30.

Ned immediately called the Total representative, apologized for d.light's delayed response, and asked to schedule a time to meet with them. The pitch was scheduled for Monday, October 26. Ned booked a flight out to Paris the next day, frantically putting together a proposal along the way.

The presentation to Total went well, bolstered by the release of the Kiran and the recent successful pilot with SKS. A few weeks later, Ned heard the good news: d.light had been selected as the supplier for the pilot project in Cameroon. Total petrol stations in the West African nation would begin selling d.light products in April 2010.

It was the company's first opportunity to work with such a large, multinational distribution partner. But it was the Total team in Cameroon that made the partnership work. "The Total team in Cameroon was exceptional," Ned explains. "We worked closely

Kenya: Creating New Freedoms

Tim Rump, d.light's first marketing director, never tired of seeing customers' reactions to the products. "The experience was always universal in the sheer and utter disbelief on the faces of people when they turned the product on," he says.

"When we'd go visit women's groups and ask women who'd bought the product to talk about their experience, the salespeople became redundant. They would gush with enthusiasm," recalls Tim. On many occasions, mothers shared how their children went from the bottom of the class to the top of the class, simply because they could study at night. Headmasters and teachers told Tim how their entire school had been transformed by access to solar-powered light, with students completing their homework, excelling at exams, and entering secondary school.

"Parents were so proud to give their kids this opportunity," Tim explains. "We used to call it 'creating new freedoms,' as people were realizing their dreams through their kids."

with them, did trainings for them on the products. They were really bought in, and they were incredibly passionate and talented."

The pilot in Cameroon went very well. With 7,400 units sold, it far outpaced the pilot in Senegal. Total invited d.light back to the bargaining table, ready to partner for a larger rollout in Africa.

It was an incredibly tough negotiation. One of the biggest points of contention was branding. Total demanded that all the solar lanterns sold through their outlets be Total branded. Ned and his team countered that the products had to carry the d.light brand; this was non-negotiable. They believed that if the d.light brand disappeared under the weight of the Total name, the deal wasn't worth it. The short-term gains in distribution and revenue were nothing compared to the long-term costs of failing to build a strong brand and reputation for d.light.

The branding dispute was resolved through an unexpected source. In parallel to the Total pilot, the d.light product design team had begun work on a branding research project in early 2010. The impetus had been a persistent problem that team members experienced whenever they met customers in the field: few people actually seemed to know what the name of the company was.

"We'd come and people would say, 'Oh, you're from the Nova company,'" Robin remembers. "We're trying to build this brand. We want customers to have confidence in our brand. But they don't even know what the brand is."

The brand confusion was exacerbated by the fact that d.light products came in multiple colors to accommodate different models and cultural preferences, including gray, red, blue, orange, and green. In addition, the Nova, Solata, and Kiran had each emerged out of separate design processes and were not

An employee at a Total service station helps market d.light products

visually related to one another. As a result, many customers didn't know they were sold by the same company. Those who did realize this tended to call the Solata and Kiran "little Novas."

"It's realistic to expect customers to only remember one word related to your brand," Ned explains. "In our case, the word everyone seemed to remember was *Nova*, not *d.light*."

After two months of intensive customer research, the design team came up with two major recommendations: manufacture all the products in the same color, regardless of geography or model; and drop product names in favor of model numbers, much like how mobile phones are typically identified. An added benefit of model numbers is that customers intuitively understand that products with higher model numbers tend to offer more features and better performance.

As a result, the Nova became the S100 and the Kiran the S10. The Solata, which had not been selling well in Tanzania and failed to sell in other markets, would no longer be produced. Both the S100 and S10, along with their packaging and accessories, became a fiery orange color, carefully chosen for its brightness, its positive cultural connotations in India and Africa, and its distinction from competitors' colors.

The new d.light brand orange also happened to resemble the corporate orange of Total. Ned brought this to the table as a compromise that all d.light products would be orange going forward but would retain the d.light brand—and, fortunately, the Total team accepted it. The two companies then moved ahead with rolling out their partnership in multiple countries across the African continent. Right away, the S100 and S10 began selling well in Total's petrol stations.

This new distribution network brought in welcome revenue for d.light, which was still struggling with its cash situation. The devastating earthquake that hit Haiti on January 12, 2010, led to another major opportunity. It was the first time that d.light was able to support disaster relief efforts at a large scale, partnering with the World Bank to send 33,000 solar lights to the hard-hit island nation.

By early 2010, Sam and Ned were actively courting Omidyar Network, an impact fund backed by eBay founder Pierre Omidyar. Their mission and values aligned well with that of d.light, and the prospect of having another strong impact investor on the board was appealing.

But the Omidyar Network was just opening up their portfolio in India and wanted to move cautiously on what would be their first investment. They conducted a long and thorough due diligence process. All the while, Sam and Ned struggled to keep the company afloat.

Then, in June 2010, six months after they had initially hoped to secure funding, they finally closed the Series B round. Omidyar Network led the round, along with additional funding from all major Series A investors, for a total of US$5.5 million.

The day the money was wired into d.light's bank account, Sam and Ned breathed a huge sigh of relief. They had been teetering on the edge of running out of cash for months, even as they expanded sales to thirty countries and reached 1.25 million customers. This infusion of funding would give the company enough runway for another couple of years.

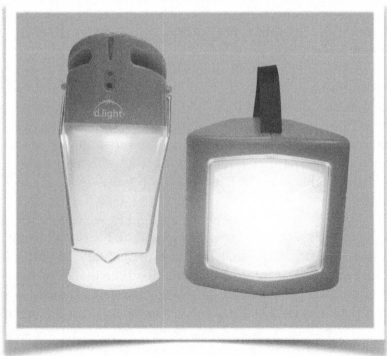

The rebranding led to all d.light products becoming orange

Chapter 16

DISTRIBUTION INNOVATIONS

By 2010, it was becoming clear that distribution was one of the biggest hurdles for d.light to overcome. For the first few years of the company, Sam and Ned had followed the advice that they consistently heard from distribution experts: sell through retail channels.

That's how everyone did it, the experts assured them. That's how a product company was built.

So they tried to sell through retail channels, pouring funding and people power toward building relationships with everyone from shop owners to large-scale FMCG retailers. But after nearly three years of grueling effort, the approach simply wasn't working. Traditional distribution models were not going to allow d.light to scale. To succeed, the team had to innovate in distribution as much as they innovated in product design.

Tanzania, where managing director Pepijn and his colleagues had struggled to gain a foothold in the market, ended up being the first place where d.light broke the mold on distribution models. This laid the groundwork for the company's future distribution strategies.

In September 2010, with his home and office still full of unsold Solatas, Pepijn called an emergency meeting with his employees.

The team, which numbered around thirty people, had sold less than half of their Solata stock in a year. They knew they were running out of time. As a company, d.light couldn't subsidize the cost of their office much longer if they couldn't sell more than their typical 5,000 units a month.

Pepijn asked his team to get as creative as possible in thinking about possible sales channels; nothing was off the table. Out of that meeting came two actionable ideas: establish a micro-finance partnership or sell to students through schools.

"Necessity was the mother of invention in this case," recalls Ned. "We were sitting on a lot of stock. Without that pressure, we may have never been forced to find more creative ways to sell."

The sales team pursued both approaches, but they quickly focused on schools when it became clear that channel had far more potential. They got connected to the association of headmasters in Tanzania, pitching the Solata to about 5,000 school headmasters from across the country. They even commissioned Mrisho Mpoto, a famous Tanzanian poet, to write and perform a song about the dangers of kerosene. The song, "Mama Siwema," became a staple on radio stations across the country.

The response from schools was incredibly enthusiastic, launching what eventually became the Right to Safe Light campaign. As part of the campaign, the team would go into a region and, with the support of the local headmaster and education government official, give a presentation directly to students. The students would take home information about the Solata to their parents, and within a week, orders would begin coming into the call center in Dar es Salaam.

The Tanzania team began the campaign on Mafia Island in October 2010, with the audacious goal of providing solar light to an entire island. They received a remarkable response: about 75 percent of households purchased a Solata, now priced at a lower 15,000 Tanzanian shillings (about US$10.70).

The Right to Safe Light campaign only grew from there. In the first month of the campaign, sales jumped to 25,000 units. And the sales kept coming. Pepijn and his team were eventually able to sell 430,000 Solatas to students across Tanzania. These Solatas provided light to around two million Tanzanians, or about 5 percent of the country's population.

Students on Mafia Island, Tanzania, at a marketing pitch for the Solata

Over the course of the campaign, as they interacted with customers, the Tanzania team was moved over and over again by how much parents valued their children's education. "Some parents would go without food so they could afford to purchase a Solata for their child to study," Pepijn recalls.

Despite the great success of the Right to Safe Light campaign, the sustainability of the Tanzania office continued to be a concern. Pepijn and his family were also facing serious personal challenges. A distributor in Tanzania had somehow gotten the false impression that Pepijn was making huge amounts of money and withholding it from his partners. She threatened Pepijn with violence, and once even showed up at the office wielding an axe. Twice, he and his family fled the country out of fear for their safety.

Eventually, Pepijn told Sam and Ned that he had to relocate his family back to the Netherlands. The best way forward, it seemed, was to shut down the d.light Tanzania office. Fortunately, a British NGO that d.light had worked closely with agreed to take over the operations of the Right to Safe Light campaign, including hiring many members of the d.light team. They would successfully continue the Right to Safe Light Campaign, providing lanterns to more than nine million people in Tanzania and other African countries.

Though this was not what Pepijn, Sam, and Ned had imagined happening when they first opened the d.light Tanzania office, there was still much to celebrate. The team's persistent efforts in Tanzania had resulted in millions of schoolchildren using a bright and safe solar lantern to study instead of a kerosene lamp, potentially transforming their entire life trajectory. It helped d.light win the prestigious Ashden Award for Sustainable Development and led to the inclusion of the d.light S250 in a British Museum exhibit and book, both entitled *A History of the World in 100 Objects*. And the work done in Tanzania was still extraordinarily valuable for d.light's overall growth. "If we hadn't done it, we wouldn't be

Papua New Guinea: Walking for Days to Buy a Solar Home System

As the managing director of global partnerships, Karl Skare has visited markets in nearly every corner of the world. "My favorite part of the job is going on field visits," he says. "It's really powerful to see the impact of the work we're doing with the beneficiaries of the products we're offering."

On one trip to Papua New Guinea in the southwestern Pacific, Karl and the distribution partner brought cartons of the D30 home system into the highlands of the island country, deep into the jungle. "There were people who had walked for multiple days in the jungle to come buy a D30," Karl remembers. "I didn't even know how people knew about it. And everyone was thanking me for bringing this great technology to them."

where we are today," Sam explains. "It put d.light on the map in Africa."

That footprint in Africa was about to get a major boost in talent. In hopes of overcoming some of the challenges around sales and distribution, Sam and Ned were recruiting more experienced sales and marketing professionals to run operations in Africa. Ned came across Tim Rump, a longtime Unilever marketing executive who had lived in several countries in Africa for two decades. Tim had specialized in marketing highly affordable Unilever products, such as shampoo in small sachets that cost only ten cents, to every village across the continent. He was in his forties but had been so successful that he had already retired back to his native United Kingdom.

By the fall of 2010, Tim was getting restless. "I was coming up on my third winter in the U.K., and it wasn't very nice," Tim remembers. He began actively looking for part-time work that would keep him busy and take him to a better climate. Then, in September, he got a call from a recruiter, pitching him a position as the managing director of Africa for d.light. Tim had no interest in being MD, but he said he'd be happy to contribute his expertise in marketing and sales. After having a phone conversation with Ned,

Tanzanian students who accessed solar lighting through the Right to Safe Light campaign

Sam, and the d.light board chair, Tim became even more excited about the opportunity.

"That was a Thursday afternoon. Then they asked, 'Can you be in Ethiopia by Saturday?'" Tim recalls, laughing. While this spontaneous approach was far removed from his Unilever experience, Tim wasn't fazed at all. "I was in a wonderful position in which I had no risks. I was retired. I was looking for something to keep me busy. Ned and Sam are highly impressive people. I'm really interested in renewable energy, interested in Africa," explains Tim. His only thought at the time was, "This is going to be a hell of a lot of fun."

After spending a week with Tim in Ethiopia to negotiate the expansion of the Total partnership in that market, Ned asked Tim to sign on as a consultant for at least a few months, but hopefully longer. "I got back to the U.K. and thought about it for about ten minutes. And then I said, 'Fine, let's give it a go,'" Tim remembers.

Soon after, the job description for the managing director position landed in the hands of David Small, a native Zimbabwean who had been a longtime sales executive at Colgate. Dave had been working in the U.K. for years but was looking for an opportunity to return to Africa. He got in touch with Ned and Sam, and met them in Hong Kong shortly afterwards.

Dave still vividly remembers that meeting—which, after years of working with large multinationals, was his first real exposure to social enterprise. "I was completely inspired by the two of them, by their vision for the future," Dave recalls. He also remembers being impressed by their willingness to admit that they needed help. "They said, 'We want this to grow big, but we know we can't do it without help. We've traveled to Africa, but we don't know it that well,'" explains Dave. "I was sold from that time."

Like Tim, Dave was asked to jump in with both feet right away. In February 2011, the day after Dave accepted the position, he met Tim for the first time at a London train station, and they both traveled to Paris to join Ned in another meeting with Total. Their partnership had been so successful that Total wanted to expand distribution to even more countries across Africa and even into Latin America. It was a "heavy negotiation," Dave remembers, but the successful end result helped poise d.light for greater growth.

Sam and Ned gave Dave the flexibility to determine where he wanted to base d.light's Africa operations. He immediately recommended Nairobi, Kenya, already a major hub for multinational corporations and NGOs in East Africa and home to a significant amount of talent. He got the go-ahead, and began working to register a d.light entity in Kenya. He found a five-bedroom home that would serve as housing for Dave, Dave's wife, Sue, and Tim, as well as the d.light office. Tim, who had never been to Kenya before, packed his bags and moved to Nairobi in April 2011.

It was d.light's second foray into Africa, and this time, they were determined to make it work.

Chapter 17

THE CASE FOR MARKETING

L ike the other offices at their inception, the new Africa team was starting from essentially nothing. Both Dave and Tim were intimately involved in all the details of getting the office set up. "I remember going to supermarkets and selecting cups and plates, and selecting carpets to help get the office up and running," Tim recalls. Having worked with a major multinational corporation for years, Tim hadn't ever done anything like this for his job. It was far outside his comfort zone. "I felt really guilty that the company was paying me to do something that was so trivial, but there was no one else to do it," he says.

They soon began hiring other team members, including Thomas Kyonze, who joined as the sales manager of East Africa. An administrative assistant, a marketing intern, and a driver followed soon after.

With the recent close of the Series B investment round, d.light's board was asking for a significant increase in revenue—and this was the charge given to Dave and his team. As a result, the new East Africa office was almost exclusively focused on sales in its first few months. "The first priority was we had to generate sales before we could think about marketing and spending money," Dave explains. "We had to solidify existing distributors and grow as quickly as we could."

The first members of the new Africa team in Nairobi, Kenya

Tim, who by now had signed on as the company's head of marketing, saw things a little differently. He thought d.light had to invest a lot more in marketing in order to grow its revenue. But as the first marketing executive d.light had ever had, Tim had to convince his colleagues that marketing was a necessary cost rather than an expense. "They had a brilliant product for a massive need," explains Tim, "but it hadn't dawned on them that people in Africa wouldn't just say, 'At last! At last!' Unless you get it in front of people and convince them that it's worth their money, it's just sitting on a production line in China."

Unfortunately, d.light didn't have the financial resources to support the kind of marketing the company needed. Tim knew that introducing customers to a new product category was most effectively done with in-person demonstrations and interactions. He had no doubt that d.light could sell significant quantities of the S10 and S300 (the latest iteration of the S100) by presenting to the many savings groups and women's groups spread out across Kenya.

But Thomas was their only sales agent, and they were trying to reach tens of millions of customers. Tim did the calculations: If he and Thomas met with three savings or women's groups a day, six days a week, it would take them 300 years to reach everyone in off-grid areas of Kenya. "That's not going to work," he remembers thinking.

As Tim was pondering this conundrum, a representative from The Shell Foundation approached d.light. The London-based foundation wanted to financially support the expansion of affordable, renewable energy solutions in Africa and Asia. They were particularly interested in directing money toward operational gaps that d.light couldn't cover. Sam and Ned connected them to Tim.

Tim briefly considered asking for funding to hire additional sales agents. But even with ten agents, it would still take them 30 years to reach the entire customer base. The company simply didn't have that kind of time. The Shell Foundation representative asked Tim, "What else would you want to do to accelerate this?" He promised funding to give Tim the freedom to experiment with different marketing strategies.

Nyanza, Kenya: A Family Transformed

Regional business manager Gawson Otieno met a family in the region of Nyanza, Kenya, whose lives were changed by the A2. They had been living on a subsistence income, surviving day by day, with nothing more than firewood to provide light for their home. When the children needed to study, they had to go to a neighbor's house.

After purchasing the A2, their daily experience changed. The adults and children could be far more productive. "We were able to address them at their point of need," Gawson explains. "For me, that was touching."

The family loved their A2 so much that they became unofficial brand ambassadors for d.light, praising the product to their friends and neighbors.

The only way to shorten the timeline, Tim knew, was to move away from push strategies and instead create pull for the products. And in Kenya, the best way to do that was to advertise through the radio. Many rural households had access to a radio, if not at home, then through neighbors or shops or the nearest town. In addition, plenty of small retailers listened to their radios while in their shops. The same advertisement could reach potential customers and distributors at the same time.

But how could they sell light through a non-visual medium? And what messaging would effectively create demand for a new type of product? Early d.light marketing efforts had focused primarily on personal and social benefits, such as reduced fumes and increased hours for work or study. From his long-term experience in rural Africa, Tim knew that such benefits weren't tangible or immediate enough. To be persuaded to part with their hard-earned money, village households had to be convinced that they were going to see instant benefits that would significantly change their lives, starting that day. Unilever, for example, couldn't sell toothpaste to base-of-the-pyramid customers by making the case for long-term dental hygiene. Customers only came flocking when the company said their products could reduce bad breath, a benefit that could be experienced right away.

So Tim decided to orient all of d.light's marketing in Kenya toward the immediate economic benefits. This was the main message he tried to communicate to potential customers: "This will give you light and cost you nothing after you purchase it. Once you've recovered the cost of buying the lantern, you will have money in your pocket every day."

This messaging was particularly effective for rural women, who were most concerned with child rearing and taking care of the household. "How do you fancy a 30 percent increase in your income every day?" the ads asked. "You could buy a goat, a bicycle, food, put a roof on the house. d.light brings that within your reach."

"And that," says Tim, "is something you can sell on the radio."

The Nairobi team began with a pilot, running one ad on one radio station. The results were "phenomenal," Tim remembers. Rural customers began asking their local retailers for the products. The retailers, who had heard the same ads, came looking for access to d.light products. Later radio advertisements would specifically

Members of a savings group in Kenya review a d.light brochure

target retailers, discussing the benefits of having a brightly lit shop that could stay open long after the sun had set.

As a numbers person, Tim meticulously tracked the resources he was investing in marketing, and the outcomes in terms of brand awareness and customer demand. The data clearly showed that marketing was a necessary cost and helped shift priorities within the company. Soon, the company's marketing budget began to grow. "Every time I gave Sam and Ned more data, they gave me more money," Tim recalls with a laugh. "They realized that the more money you spend on marketing, you generate more sales."

The Africa team still had to work within real budget constraints, though. Dave remembers having to think about this on a daily basis, wondering how ongoing operations could be conducted in the most cost-efficient manner. They strategically went after partners that already had existing distribution networks to minimize the resources d.light would have to put into the partnership. When the product design team came from Hong Kong to Nairobi for customer research on what would become the S1, they all stayed in the spare rooms of the office. Whenever they went out into the field, they found low-cost lodgings and shared rooms.

Though it wasn't always easy to keep costs low, Dave loved what this said about d.light's values and priorities as an organization. "No one cared that this was where we were at. We were doing such a fantastic thing. When we were in the field, we saw the impact. That's far more important than numbers. We saw impact."

Thankfully, both the numbers and the impact grew. As the team's work in Kenya began to show promising results, they looked elsewhere in the continent for opportunities, especially in Tanzania, Rwanda, Burundi, and Ethiopia. Eventually, they opened a new sales office in Lagos, Nigeria, to support sales in West Africa.

The newly revitalized Africa operations were off to a promising start. But just as they were gaining steam, Sam and Ned realized they were running on empty. After more than four years of giving everything they had to d.light, the co-founders were exhausted and overwhelmed. Their desire to share the leadership burden with someone else would lead to a consequential decision—and, eventually, some of the greatest challenges ever faced by d.light.

Chapter 18

NEW LEADERSHIP

In early 2011, Sam and Ned were on the verge of burnout. They had both lived overseas since 2008, traveled hundreds of thousands of miles, raised three rounds of investment, started four international offices, and worked countless hours.

They were also feeling unsure of their ability to lead the company to the next level. They hadn't yet been able to hit the US$5 price point for a solar lantern that they had been dreaming about from d.light's founding. The offices in China, India, and Kenya were growing rapidly and needed increasingly robust systems and processes. Investors were asking for continued expansion and tangible financial results. And, at 3 million customers, they were still a long way off from the 100 million customer goal that had been set for 2020.

One day in Hong Kong, the two founders met together and realized they were both thinking the same thing: it was time to bring in new leadership.

"If there's someone who can grow d.light faster than we can, if our ability to grow it is a limiting factor on the business, then why not bring in someone else?" Sam remembers thinking. They wanted someone with far more experience managing large companies through rapid growth. They also wanted someone to help share the load of responsibilities that Sam and Ned had been carrying for so many years. Both of them intended to remain on the executive leadership team, but they thought bringing in a different CEO would benefit the company.

In the end, they didn't need to look far. A longtime adviser to d.light with extensive executive leadership experience expressed interest in becoming CEO. It seemed like the perfect solution: he was already familiar with d.light; Sam and Ned had worked closely with him; and it would save the company from having to do an extensive, and expensive, search.

In March 2011, the co-founders sent all d.light employees an open letter. The first paragraph stated, "Since the beginning, we have been clear with our board and investors that at some point we would ask for a seasoned CEO to ensure we meet d.light's ambitious goals. That time has come, and the board has supported our request." Sam would move to the role of chief customer officer; Ned would remain as president.

In the first year after the transition, business seemed to continue as usual with d.light. The company released its newest and lowest cost product, the S1 study light, on May 18, 2011. This, according to Xian, was when the product design team "really hit it out of the park." Now located in Hong Kong, the design team had been able to collaborate far more closely with the engineers and contract manufacturers to reduce costs as much as possible.

"We were a bit obsessive about it," Robin, the head of product design, recalls. The team cut every cent possible out of production costs. When they found a way to reduce the cost as much as five to ten cents, they would have a major celebration. The product development process also became much more efficient, going from fifteen months for the S10 to less than nine months for the S1.

While the S10 had been positioned as a competitor to the kerosene lantern, the S1 was meant to replace candles or divvy lamps, which were often nothing more than small bottles with kerosene wicks. Many children in off-grid households tended to use these divvy lamps to study, and that's exactly whom the designers had in mind when they created the small, disc-shaped S1.

Robin clearly remembers visiting a home in India while testing the S10, and observing a young boy as he studied with a divvy lamp. When they swapped it for an S10, the boy's demeanor and

Rift Valley, Kenya: Going the Extra Mile in After-Sales Service

Regional business manager Daisy Jeruto and her team frequently help install home systems for customers in her territory of the south Rift Valley—and Daisy doesn't let wearing a skirt stop her.

"The clients are so excited to buy the kit. My best time is going on the roof and helping to install the solar," she says. "And seeing the light in the evening, that's the best thing. Then you see the kids come and you see their excitement."

Once, a customer had trouble getting reception for his d.light television. He lived in a very rural area near Maasai Mara National Reserve, where there were no paved roads. Daisy and her colleague rode a motorbike to the customer's home through a rainstorm. After arriving, they figured out that the customer needed to extend his antenna.

"We had to cut down a tree, and it was nine at night," Daisy remembers. "We cut down a tree, got a long stick, and then we went up on the roof to put it up." The signal for the TV was finally clear, and the customer's children, seeing a television program for the first time, were delighted.

Students in India react with joy at receiving S1 lanterns to help them study

posture immediately transformed. He was able to sit up straighter; his eyes were more focused and he breathed more easily. "I realized this child really needs this," Robin remembers. But the price point of the S10 was far out of reach for the boy's family. "We didn't have the right product for him yet."

The S1 was that product, retailing at about US$8, or two-thirds the cost of the S10. It was intentionally designed as a very simple, easy-to-use product with only one function—light—that it did very well. But the product's small form factor didn't mean that it was any less durable. In early testing, the China team went so far as to drive over an S1 with a four-door sedan. The little study light survived with just a couple cracks, and still worked perfectly.

Especially in East Africa, the S1 was an immediate hit. The company was selling fifteen to twenty thousand units a month worldwide, with most of those sales happening in Africa. "It was a superb product," says Dave Small. He thought the S1 represented d.light's core value for customers well: "Just because you're poor, it doesn't mean we can't give you the best."

With growing operations in Africa, India, and China, and a newly established headquarters in San Francisco, California, an executive team was formalized. They met in a different region each quarter. "We got to know different countries, different heads of departments," Dave recalls. "We made decisions as a team on very strategic things."

One time, the executives had a tough decision to make about where d.light's limited financial resources should be allocated. Jaideep Mukherji, then the managing director of Asia, advocated for more money for product development rather than the field offices. Dave agreed with him, and the executives as a whole supported that decision. This, to Dave, exemplified how the leadership prioritized the well-being of the company over their own spheres of work.

"We had two years of great growth and great teamwork," Dave says. During that time, the new CEO hired other highly experienced managers; his leadership enabled Sam, and Ned and his wife to move back to North America. This gave the founders the space to pursue major life changes. Ned and Dorcas had their first child; Sam married a college friend named Rosie.

The CEO successfully raised US$11 million in a Series C round led by Draper Fisher Jurvetson and Omidyar Network. The company continued to grow and the products continued to sell well, with the number of people impacted surpassing 10 million. In addition, d.light won some significant recognitions, including the US$1.5 million Zayed Future Energy Award and the Verizon Powerful Answers Award.

Maasai children in Kenya study by the light of their S1s

This was also the point at which the d.light team finally figured out a solution to the longstanding challenge of distribution in India. In the summer of 2013, three business school students—one from Stanford, another from Harvard, and the third from UC Berkeley's Haas School of Business—traveled to Kenya, Latin America, and India, respectively, to explore consumer financing options and to recommend pilot projects to pursue. After weeks of research, the students came back to the leadership with one clear recommendation: d.light had to partner with micro-finance institutions.

The obvious market for the pilot was India, where, after a few years of turmoil and conflict with the state government of Andhra Pradesh, the micro-finance industry had emerged even stronger than before.[14] In addition to specializing in consumer loans, the industry had immense reach into rural areas and relatively high levels of trust among base-of-the-pyramid families. A successful collaboration could break open the market at an unprecedented scale.

Managing director Jaideep Mukherji hired someone with a long history of working with micro-finance institutions to be the new MFI channel head for d.light. This manager, along with the sales team, went back to SKS Microfinance with a proposal for a new partnership. With the maturation of d.light's brand and the micro-finance sector as a whole, SKS readily agreed to a large-scale cross-sales partnership with d.light. Other MFIs soon followed suit.

Suddenly, the S300 and S10 began selling in India at rates the team had never seen before. As affordability increased and risk decreased for customers, a large new lower-income market segment opened up to d.light. "We were getting 20 to 30 percent conversion rates of customers who were pitched the product," Ned remembers. "Sometimes we were selling more than 100,000 units a month through the MFIs." This was a big reason why d.light was able to reach the milestone of impacting 25 million people by early 2014.

The success of the MFI partnerships brought home the reality that financing was essential to the future success of d.light. "We often talk about how our customers are constrained," Sam says. "For most of our history, we talked of power being the constraint, and once that's removed, a lot can happen for customers. But we've learned that financial constraints are just as important. If we can

A large women's group in India proudly show off their new S10 lanterns

remove this, then we open up the door to power and other needs for customers."

But collaborating with MFIs wasn't necessarily a replicable strategy. Micro-finance institutions were not as prevalent in other regions of the world. In Africa, existing micro-finance organizations operated at a small scale and the vast majority of the population remained unbanked. So, what would it look like to bring a consumer financing model to Africa?

Ned and Sam had already been dreaming about this possibility since at least 2010. At that time, mobile money was revolutionizing financial services for base-of-the-pyramid families in Africa, turning mobile phones into bank accounts and enabling digital payments. M-Pesa, a mobile phone-based money transfer and payment service launched by Vodafone in East Africa, was already the most successful mobile phone-based financial service in the developing world. In Kenya alone, the M-Pesa mobile money app had 17 million subscribers by December 2011.[15]

Back then, the idea of directly doing consumer financing—on top of the extensive work being done in product development, sales, and distribution—felt overwhelming. But the movement toward digital money prompted Sam and Ned, along with then head of engineering Doug Ricket, to do some initial design work on a system that collected payments through mobile money. Perhaps, they thought, there was a way to remotely activate or shut down products based on customers' payments. They experimented with various ideas and even submitted a few patents that would end up being the foundation for future pay-as-you-go systems.

In 2013, d.light began to partner with another venture-backed company based in Kenya, which was providing consumer financing for solar home systems. The D10 home system, designed by d.light, was sold through the partner's distribution network, with customers paying US$25 as a down payment and then fifty cents a day for about a year.

The rapid growth of this project was further proof that solar home systems, coupled with affordable consumer financing, were a winning combination. So winning, in fact, that both d.light and the partner became interested in doing pay-go solar on their own. They parted ways in March 2014.

Soon after, Karl Skare was brought on board as the product manager for pay-go products. He led a pilot of d.light's first prototype solar home system in Haiti that relied on the pay-as-you-go methodology. When customers submitted a payment via their mobile phone, their home system would be remotely unlocked via a GSM chip.

The pilot was a bit of "a disaster," says Karl, in part because d.light and its Haitian partner could not agree on pretty much every aspect of the pay-go strategy, from pricing to after-sales service. On top of that, the GSM chip in the system didn't always work as it was supposed to. Even so, "I had clarity that this was the future," Karl remembers. He presented to the d.light executive team, asking that they continue to pursue pay-go but with more control of the customer experience. Based on customer research, he recommended a keypad instead of GSM and a lease-to-own model rather than a service model. His presentation prompted a lively debate and discussion around the work needed to transition to a keypad system.

How the next iteration of the home system would function was a minor issue compared to the challenges that were on the horizon for d.light. The entire company, it turns out, would soon reach the brink of collapse—and only immense sacrifice, risk, and dedication would bring it back to life.

Chapter 19

A round 2013, the culture of d.light had begun to shift. The regional offices began to feel increasingly cut off from the San Francisco-based executives, disempowered to contribute to the company's strategic direction. The office in Hong Kong was closed. The product pipeline stagnated.

As the vision for a three-person leadership model began to fall apart, Sam felt increasingly pushed out of the company. He began to reduce his time on the job. During 2013 to 2014, he went from full time to eventually only 20 percent time at d.light, taking on consulting projects with other solar companies. "If I'm not uniquely valuable to d.light, then I should do whatever I can best do for the world," he thought at the time. Several other key leaders, including co-founder Xian Wu, head of product design Robin Chilton, Africa managing director Dave Small, and Asia managing director Jaideep Mukherji, clashed with the leadership and eventually left.

By the end of 2014, the red flags had begun to emerge in earnest. The company was experiencing significant turnover, and many of the departing employees were seeking out Sam and Ned to express their concerns. Operational expenses were ballooning out of control; product development had no clear direction; team morale was low

Rajasthan, India: Fanning Happiness

A service manager with d.light India, Ritesh Mahajan often gets to deliver new products to customers. He once brought a solar fan to a family in the state of Rajasthan in northern India and was enthusiastically greeted by the family. The father told Ritesh that they experienced frequent power cuts, which made life challenging for his children, especially during the hot summers.

Now, with a solar-powered fan, their daily lives would change dramatically. "The happiness I have seen on the face of those children, and the shine in their eyes when I brought the fan to their place—that was unforgettable to me," remembers Ritesh.

and good people were leaving. The company was transforming into an unrecognizable organization.

The two co-founders came together to strategize about what they should do. They interviewed departing employees, dug into the numbers, and began engaging board members.

As far as Ned and Sam were concerned, there was only one option left: they had to take back leadership of the company.

Ned was honest with Sam about what this required. "If we're going to do this, we have to do it together. You have to come back full time," he told Sam.

It didn't take long for Sam to agree. "A lot of my life and passion and energy had gone into d.light. I didn't want it to go down," he says. And the other enterprises he was supporting didn't have the same potential for large-scale impact that d.light had. "A trusted coach advised me, 'Probably the biggest impact you can have is to go back to d.light and help it realize its full potential.'"

On March 1, 2015, several months after Sam and Ned had first grown extremely concerned and one month after they had taken those concerns to the board, the CEO and d.light mutually parted ways. Ned was installed as the interim CEO and Sam as chief product officer. The longtime business partners had no issues with switching roles. "It seemed only logical," Sam explains of his decision not to ask for the CEO position back. "Ned had stayed with the company. Everyone knew him and was really supportive of him."

When Ned and Sam took over the reins of d.light, the company was in serious trouble. The company was burning US$1.7 million in cash every month; it had only a few months of cash runway before bankruptcy. To make matters even more alarming, d.light owed a total of US$5 million in loan repayments to two separate banks before the end of the year. The banks had every right to request early paybacks of their loans in light of the situation, which would have immediately bankrupted the company. To keep d.light alive, the first priorities were to make some major cuts—quickly—and ask the banks for time to turn things around.

The day after he became CEO, Ned cut eight of the company's ten other executives, most of whom were based in San Francisco. He then traveled to India to meet with the remaining key leaders— Sam, the CFO, the managing director of global sales, the financial controller, the China general manager, and product manager Karl Skare—for an emergency meeting on how to proceed. The situation that Ned laid out was dire. "This is a do-or-die situation," Karl remembers thinking. "This will have to be a complete turnaround."

The entire leadership team agreed to immediate voluntary salary reductions. They also agreed that major staffing cuts would need to be made in the cost centers, San Francisco and China. A hiring freeze was implemented in the other offices and any non-essential projects were put on hold.

While in India, Ned heard more bad news. The managing director of global sales told him that a major distribution partner was about to end their partnership with d.light. The partner had been promised a new product by d.light months ago, but it had never come. They were now fed up and threatening to move their business to one of d.light's competitors unless they received the promised product in less than a month.

At that time, this single partner provided up to 50 percent of d.light's revenue. If they left, this would spell the end of the company. It was one more serious threat to add to an already long list of threats they were facing.

The level of anxiety and stress that Ned shouldered during that time was almost unbearable. "It's that feeling that your insides are being chewed out. You feel like you can't do it, but there's no one else," he remembers. "We were staring at the brink of failure. Every minute was hard. There was no break. My mind was always thinking about it. Even when I slept or ate, I was still thinking about it." This was, by far, the most difficult season in his eight years with d.light. During that time, he leaned heavily on Sam, whom he saw as a close friend, not just a business partner, and on board chair Stuart Davidson. The two provided invaluable support and mentorship on a near daily basis.

After spending a couple of days in India, Ned flew directly to China to lay off more than one-third of the employees there. Ned addressed the entire China team first. "I told them I was sorry that this had happened. I said I had let go of most of the executive team," Ned recalls. "And then I told them it wasn't their fault. They had done a good job. It's just what we had to do to save the company."

There were many tears, but those whose positions had been cut understood why the decision had been made. Ned remembers how much care the China employees put into closing out their projects

The Shenzhen, China, office in 2015

and making sure that their work was handed off to colleagues. Some even came in the next day, voluntarily and on their own time, to help ensure a smooth transition. "They cared so much about the mission of the company," explains Ned. "Even thinking about it today, it makes me tear up and I'm so appreciative."

He promised the China employees who were losing their jobs that d.light would help them find other work. And the human resources team in China did just that, working around the clock to support their former colleagues' job searches.

The same day the China team was reduced, the CFO returned to the San Francisco office with the task of cutting 80 percent of the team there. Ned spoke to the team via video conference from China, once again explaining the situation and apologizing to those who would lose their jobs. The CFO handled the individual conversations.

Jacob Lewandowski, then the product manager of customer interaction systems, remembers that day vividly. At the start of the morning, the office had fifteen employees, including finance specialists, product designers, and engineers. Within one hour, only he, product designer Eva Hoffmann, and the CFO remained. In the weeks that followed, the San Francisco office space—along with its sky-high rent—was shut down altogether.

In addition to having to reduce operational expenses as much as possible, the team also had to preserve d.light's existing revenue. The remaining product and engineering employees in China were given a nearly impossible task: come up with a brand-new product for the distribution partner that was threatening to walk, and do it in only three weeks. Ned told them the company was depending on them; d.light would not survive if they couldn't deliver.

Sam was tasked with overseeing the work of the China team and ensuring they stayed focused. "Previously we had dozens of projects going on, way more than they could handle. We needed to pare back," he recalls. Being put in this high-stakes situation certainly helped the team narrow down their priorities.

About a week after becoming CEO, Ned flew back to the U.S. It was time to address the next threat on the list: the banks and the US$5 million in loans that d.light owed before the end of the year. He scheduled urgent meetings with both lenders in order to buy more time.

Ned and the CFO walked into those meetings with a detailed plan to save the company. They were upfront about d.light's current challenges but also explained exactly how they were going to turn things around. "We need you to be patient," Ned remembers requesting. He committed to paying back the full US$5 million by the end of 2015, as long as they would give him time to fix things. Amazingly, both banks expressed support for the mission of d.light and agreed to wait.

Before the end of March, less than a month after the start of the turnaround, the China team indeed delivered a new product. "They figured out how to get the product launched," Ned explains. "They focused all their energy on that one project." The team had created an upgraded version of the S300, calling it the S450. The packaging and marketing materials were all revamped and refreshed. The first units of the S450 came off the production line and were immediately air-shipped to the distribution partner.

The d.light team waited anxiously to hear feedback. When the news came, it was overwhelmingly positive: The distributor loved the new product, as did their customers. They were happy to continue working with d.light.

It was a major victory worth celebrating. But d.light still had a long road ahead.

The Nairobi, Kenya, office in 2016

Chapter 20

THE $5 LANTERN

Despite the intense hardship and stress of saving d.light from the brink of collapse, there was renewed energy and focus in the remaining members of the team. "I remember feeling depressed but also energized," Sam reflects. "I'm the kind of person who responds to challenge and having the ability to make things happen. It was energizing to shed the pity and get out and figure out how to turn around the company step by step."

Every individual within the company had to step up. Many worked long days and weekends. Others volunteered to take salary cuts. Some former employees got in touch with Ned and Sam, asking what they could do to help. "It was a really bonding experience," says Karl. "I found those times quite exhilarating, knowing that if you didn't do everything in your power to help, the company might go bankrupt." In May 2015, amidst all the chaos, d.light managed to reach its 50 millionth customer.

Not everyone wanted to stay. The chief financial officer left. Those who thought the company was doomed headed for the exits soon after.

Ned and Sam needed someone to fill the CFO role—and soon. They looked to India with the hopes of finding someone who was in the market with d.light's customers and could be more personally

The China team celebrates impacting 50 million lives

connected to the mission. An investor introduced Ned to Kamal Lath, an experienced financial executive in Mumbai who was about to accept a job with another firm.

The situation that Ned laid out before Kamal wasn't exactly attractive: a relatively young company just starting to come back from near bankruptcy, with anxious lenders and investors that required managing, and the need for new investors willing to take a chance on a struggling venture. Financially, d.light was not in a position to compete with Kamal's other offer. On top of that, the job would require Kamal and his family to relocate to New Delhi, disrupting their established lives in Mumbai.

Kamal talked to his family about the possibility of moving, and other challenges that might come with the job. After hearing about the work of d.light, his wife, Oorjita, urged him to join. Kamal remembers thinking, "The needs of the rural people weren't being met. The mission was really important. And I liked being able to work with the founders. They were so passionate about the mission." Though the decision in many ways didn't make sense, Kamal chose to accept the job as d.light's CFO.

When Kamal started on July 1, 2015, the company's operations were still in disarray. The first time he looked at d.light's balance sheet and saw the grave financial situation in detail, he nearly fell out of his chair. It was clear that he had taken on a herculean task. But Kamal had no regrets. "It never occurred to me to reconsider my decision," he says. "With each challenge that I saw, my resilience was only enhanced."

Shortly after, d.light received an additional infusion of bridge funding from existing investors, led by Acumen and Omidyar. In particular, Stuart Davidson, who represented Acumen on the board, and Matt Bannick of Omidyar were strong advocates for the company's resiliency, eventually convincing every investor to provide money to keep d.light afloat.

While the most immediate threats to d.light's survival had been held off, there were still very real existential threats that could kill the company over time. "There was a big risk that we could do all this work, save the company, and then have d.light die a slow death," Ned explains.

Even with its very limited resources, d.light had to plan for the future in a rapidly changing industry. All of the existing players in the off-grid energy space were moving their attention to financed solar home systems, and new competitors were popping up all the time. "The whole industry was shifting. We had to not just move with it but be leaders in it," says Ned.

But offering financing to customers at scale required cash in the form of a fresh infusion of equity—and lots of it. No funder was going to want to touch d.light while the company was in such a financially fragile place. According to Ned, "We had to get enough proof points to raise equity to pivot the company."

Their first major, seemingly counterintuitive move was to release the A1, which had been in development for more than a year. With the support of designers from renowned design firm IDEO, the design team had finally hit that magic retail price point of US$5, which was affordable even to families making as little as US$1.25 a day. At that price, the product would pay for itself in less than three weeks in many of d.light's core markets.

But spending any resources to launch the A1 was risky. At such a low price, d.light was making minimal margin on each unit. The broader industry saw solar lamps as an increasingly irrelevant technology; many investors no longer had an interest in funding companies that focused on solar lamps.

For these reasons, the A1 almost wasn't completed. The former executive team had put a hold on the A1, concerned that the team wasn't meeting their cost targets and the A1 might cannibalize d.light's other products, particularly the S1 and S10. But product designer Eva Hoffmann, in partnership with a mechanical engineer in China, quietly persevered. "So much of my work was already done that it felt silly not to keep pushing it forward," Eva explains. "So we kept it going in the background, letting the conversations keep going. It wasn't costing much time or manpower."

When Ned took over as CEO, their efforts had resulted in a product that was pretty much ready for market. Eva and her colleagues had found dozens of creative ways to cut costs from the A1, including working with lower-cost suppliers and manufacturers, reducing unnecessary efficiencies from the solar panel, and switching to a glue that dried more quickly, increasing the speed of production.

Even though the off-grid industry was focused on home systems, Ned was certain that d.light had to release the A1. "We were putting a stake in the ground on our mission and impact. Over the past few years, people were getting confused about the focus of the company. This, having a US$5 solar light, was what was in our original business plan. By principle, we wanted to launch the product," Ned explains.

The launch of the A1 sent a clear message that d.light was still prioritizing the needs of base-of-the-pyramid customers. It still had the same mission as it had from day one. Ned and Sam wanted

Sam and a distribution partner with President Barack Obama at an event to launch the A1

partners and customers to know this, but the message was also for employees. "This was a big rallying moment for our company," Ned says. "There was an energy that was created when the A1 came out. It was the beginning of our rebirth."

The launch of the A1 on July 8, 2015, was also highly strategic. At long last, d.light had developed a product that was so affordable that it could reach an unprecedented scale of off-grid families, freeing them from kerosene and giving them the opportunity to switch to renewable energy. This would greatly strengthen the d.light brand and establish a far broader base of loyal customers. "That product is a brand builder," Sam explains. "After people have a fantastic experience with d.light with an entry-level product, what do they do next?" With the money that A1 customers save from no longer having to use kerosene, they could very well choose to purchase other d.light products.

"We believed strongly in the idea of the energy access ladder. From our research and experience, we knew that once customers had a good experience with an entry-level solar product, they would want to continue to upgrade to bigger and better products," explains Ned. Rather than cannibalizing d.light's product line, the A1 would open up the market for them, allowing a far greater number of households to step onto the first rung of the energy access ladder.

Another way in which d.light leaders wanted to help rebuild the company was through reasserting its organizational values. From the beginning, the culture of the company had always been essential to the founders. Former global human resources director Harry Wang, who first joined d.light as the human resources manager in China in 2009, remembers how organizational culture was one of the first areas he and Ned discussed. "When I first joined, I thought the company was too small to have a culture. The whole China office was smaller than the office I had when I worked at Ernst & Young," Harry recalls. "But Ned was very insistent we had to talk about culture every year. It wasn't until my third year that I realized this was necessary. And then I saw that the culture had been there all along."

In their annual executive strategy session that year, company leaders had to tackle all kinds of tough decisions around budgeting, staffing, and strategic planning. Afterwards, according to Harry,

The A1 is distributed in Banswara, India

"we rewarded ourselves with a culture discussion." Coming out of such a challenging staffing season—full of transitions, departures, and layoffs—had made the management team realize that good people were not something to be taken for granted. And figuring out exactly what characteristics allowed some employees to thrive more than others could be highly valuable and strategic information.

That hours-long conversation led to the creation of the i.HOPE values: Innovation, Honesty, Optimism, Passion, and Empathy. They were the most memorable iteration of corporate values that d.light had had since its founding. Harry and his team were given the charge of coming up with value behavior traits to define how each value could actually be embodied on a day-to-day basis, which eventually led to a vibrant system of incentives and rewards for employees who live out the d.light values in exceptional ways.

This conversation about organizational culture was facilitated by the fact that d.light was finally on firmer financial ground. By July 2015, the company broke even—a remarkable turnaround from its US$1.7 million per-month deficit from earlier in the year. In September 2015, d.light actually made a small profit. And the company was able to keep its commitments to lenders, paying back every cent of the US$5 million due at the end of the year.

But this wasn't enough. To scale up a pay-as-you-go product, which essentially provided loans to customers, the company needed more equity and a strategy that would ensure d.light's market leadership for years to come. Even with the A1, the existing product line wasn't going to sustain and grow the company in the long run. Just like the rest of the industry, they were going to have to pivot to pay-go, and they had to figure out how to do it on a shoestring budget.

Kenya: The d.light Village

In an effort to live out d.light's I.HOPE values outside of the office, employees in Kenya have used national holidays as an opportunity to serve their community. On one such occasion, regional business manager Nixon Timbit and his team built a house for an elderly man whose mud home had collapsed.

This man happened to live in a village called Kambi Giza, which means *dark village* in Kiswahili. When Nixon and his colleagues learned of this, they decided to raise money out of their own pockets to provide 300 S3s for every family in the village.

The community decided to change its name to Kambi d.light, or *d.light village*, as they are no longer living in the dark. "When we went out there, it was celebrations and tears everywhere," Nixon remembers. "This is what I think d.light stands for: changing people's lives."

Chapter 21

W hen the majority of the San Francisco-based team was cut in March 2015, much of the design and engineering efforts that had already gone into pay-go were at risk of being permanently lost. A financed solar home system was far more complex than any of d.light's previous product offerings. Customers would pay daily fees through mobile money and then receive a text with a code to be entered into the control box to unlock it. If customers didn't make a payment on time, the system would lock and not power any of the devices.

The firmware in the control boxes was critical for controlling the locking and unlocking, and preventing hacks or other security risks. On top of this, engineers had been developing a comprehensive cloud-based platform called Atlas to track all registrations and transactions to ensure that customers received the services they paid for.

Pay-go could only work if the control box and Atlas platform worked. But all this was at risk when the software engineers were let go. Retaining the intellectual property and coding related to pay-go became a top priority.

Ned asked product manager Jacob Lewandowski to track down external consultants and his former colleagues to collect the necessary code and information for pay-go and Atlas to move forward. Ned gave Jacob six months and almost no budget.

Jacob certainly felt the weight of the task assigned to him. "The market was shifting toward home systems. We were worried that we were being left behind," he recalls. "I felt like I had to make pay-go work, or d.light is dead."

The first d.light-branded solar home system had been under development for years. Once the partnership with the Kenyan consumer financing firm dissolved in 2014, the company began pursuing the project in earnest. While the product designers and engineers had been simultaneously working on a higher-end system, called the X850, and a more affordable entry-level system, the D30, the decision was made to put the X-series on hold and launch the D30 first.

"We needed to prove ourselves in the entry-level systems before we could raise capital to provide larger home systems," Karl explains. The bigger the system, the more upfront costs d.light would have to shoulder. Given their financial challenges, they had to choose the less expensive option.

The original schedule had been to launch the D30 in Kenya in June 2015, but with all the setbacks they had experienced during the leadership transition, that was no longer realistic. The new goal was to introduce the product before the end of the year.

For that to happen, Jacob had to retrieve key information from former employees. This included everything from the circuit design of the control box to important security features that would prevent hacking, as well as the code for Atlas.

Convincing recently laid off employees to spend additional time transferring knowledge and files wasn't an easy task. The contractor who had been hired to code the Atlas platform was also unresponsive. According to Jacob, "The contractor was not getting me the info I needed. Then he just stops working, stops communicating with me. Then I have to try to get our money back from him."

Over the next few months, Jacob tracked down the former firmware engineer and got him to transfer the code. As he neared his deadline, Jacob ended up chasing d.light's former CTO all the way to another state—to Portland, Oregon—where the CTO had moved shortly after leaving the company. "I got him to agree to

India: Boosting Business for a Rural Restaurant

During a customer research trip, India managing director Kamal Lath met a couple who lived in a home deep inside the forest, at least 300 meters from their nearest neighbor. With no electricity, they were accustomed to being in complete darkness at night.

The couple also owned a small restaurant that was about twelve feet square and had only two tables for customers. They purchased a D30 home system to light their restaurant. When Kamal visited them, the restaurant was extremely busy with more than thirty customers—many of whom had been attracted by the bright lights.

"The restaurant owner joined our pitch to tell the customers how the light was so good," Kamal remembers. "We got ten registrations right there."

The woman also shared how her life had been transformed since purchasing the home system. She told Kamal, "My husband respects me more. He can't serve so many customers, so he needs my help. We've been able to save money to send our children to school."

spend a Saturday morning with us in Portland," Jacob remembers. "I flew three consultant engineers from Europe to San Francisco. Then we went to Portland together." The four of them, along with the former CTO, crowded into a low-budget hotel room. Over the course of several hours, the former CTO walked them through the existing code as they furiously took notes.

Jacob successfully delivered all the necessary information by September 2015. Two months later, after an intense scramble by consultants, manufacturers, and d.light team members, the D30 was launched on a small scale in Embu County, a predominantly rural region in central Kenya with a population of around 500,000. Embu had been mostly overlooked by other competitors, so it was the perfect place to run a pilot of the pay-go home system and all the infrastructure around it.

"We wanted to see if we could get the model working," Ned explains. "There were many pieces to build: distribution, collections, tracking inventory because we were putting lots of expensive products out there, servicing, the backend software and infrastructure, encryption."

It was a gamble. While most companies on the brink of collapse tend to shrink their operations, d.light was expanding into an entirely new product line, one that would require significant capital to scale. As a result, the pay-go strategy faced internal and external detractors. Ned remembers receiving angry emails from some investors and board members, urging him to stick with portable lanterns. Even d.light's own managing director of global sales wasn't convinced. Despite their objections, Ned and Sam were confident that this was the way forward for the company.

At this time, many players in the off-grid energy industry had already written off d.light. Ned decided to encourage that perception and use it to their advantage. If competitors didn't see d.light as a threat, they wouldn't pay attention to the rollout of the D30 pilot. "If a competitor came and messed up our pilot, we would have been finished. If someone else came into Embu, we didn't have the resources to fight against it," Ned remembers. By staying under the radar, d.light could lay the groundwork for the next stage of the company without being challenged.

On November 24, 2015, d.light registered its first pay-go customer. Jacob still remembers that instant. He was sitting in a taxi

Employees in Kenya help the first ever D30 customer install his system

on his way to the Nairobi airport, preparing to go back to the U.S., when the notification came on his phone. He quickly sent an exuberant email to Ned, Sam, and others. It was an electric moment.

The pilot launch, which also eventually encompassed Machakos County near Nairobi, hit some rough patches. Customers didn't always receive an unlock code after making a payment. The backend system had some bugs. Some of the initial salespeople weren't a good fit and had to be replaced.

Overall, though, early customer response to the D30 in Embu and Machakos was incredibly positive. Consumers were more than happy to pay the US$20 deposit and 40 cents a day for multiple lights, phone charging, a torch, and a radio that they would fully own after a year. The radio was particularly significant, as it marked d.light's first major foray into a product category other than light— and it made customers eager to access other solar-powered appliances.

But there was much more to do to develop a significant enough track record to attract investors so d.light could scale across Kenya and beyond. They had tried to build up the pay-go sales and after-sales infrastructure with a minimal number of team members, but it soon became clear that this product offering required considerably more manpower than the solar lanterns. It also didn't help that, after

Dave Small's departure, there hadn't been any managing director in Africa.

With the future of the company still at risk, Ned felt the need to make a big investment in the Kenya office. In April 2016, he temporarily relocated with his wife and three-year-old son to Nairobi so he could support D30 sales and marketing, hire a new managing director for Africa, and court investors.

Now officially appointed by the board as CEO, Ned had been speaking to investors to try to raise a Series D round. But he kept encountering one closed door after another. "Every investor thought that d.light was over," he remembers. "They preferred newer companies without baggage and with nice press coverage. They didn't like solar lanterns anymore." Being honest about d.light's recent challenges while also pitching their strategy to regain industry leadership was a hard sell. "Investors would be interested, but then they would invest in our competitors," explains Ned.

What Ned really needed was time—time to demonstrate that d.light was recovering well and could lead the market in both portable solar lanterns and pay-go home systems. He knew that d.light had a strong team with excellent products, production

Ned and his son in Nairobi

capabilities, and distribution networks. But the company had minimal experience extending financing and credit to customers, and those on the outside needed to be convinced of their long-term viability.

The clearest proof point would be running an unquestionably successful pilot of the D30 in Kenya with very limited resources and in a market that was becoming increasingly crowded. In a very real way, the future of the company depended on the success of the D30.

With Ned on the ground, and bolstered frontline staff and leadership in Kenya, the pilot results showed more and more promise. And as d.light's financial outlook improved, so did their chances of securing additional funding. Existing funder NewQuest Capital Partners offered to provide additional funding first, on the assumption that Ned could secure other investors. KawaSafi Ventures Fund, a new offshoot of Acumen that was focused on energy, and Energy Access Ventures, an energy-focused investor in Africa, agreed to put money in too. Omidyar Network also decided to add to their stake in the company.

Even then, the deal almost fell apart. The existing investors and new investors had trouble agreeing on the final terms. d.light was once again at risk of running out of cash. The cash-intensive pay-go model, while clearly the future of the company, drained its bank accounts far more quickly than the solar lanterns ever had.

For a few days, it was touch and go, with one investor threatening to walk away and another threatening to let d.light go bankrupt. It was a horrible time for Ned, during which he barely ate or slept. "I don't think I could have survived on my own then," he remembers. "I really needed help from others." Ned turned to a few close friends for ongoing prayer and encouragement, including co-founder Xian Wu, who was no longer with the company but was still actively rooting for its success.

Finally, after many tense back-and-forths among all the parties involved, Jacqueline Novogratz, the CEO of Acumen, personally intervened and ensured that the deal went through.

On a mild Saturday morning in September 2016, as Ned watched his son play in a swimming pool at a Nairobi hotel, he finally got the phone call he had been waiting one and a half years for: the investors had all signed the term sheet. The company was about to receive US$15 million in equity, along with US$2.5 million in debt financing from SunFunder and US$5 million in grants from philanthropic and development organizations.

"For the first time in a year and a half, I felt this peace," Ned remembers. "We had done it. That was the end of the turnaround chapter. We could move on. It felt amazing."

A woman in Kenya cooks by the light of a D30

Chapter 22

Around the time of the close of Series D, Ned officially handed off leadership of d.light's Africa operations to Jacob Okoth, a Kenya native with more than fifteen years of operational experience in several sectors, including insurance, fast-moving consumer goods, and telecommunications. Jacob and his family had been living in Kampala, Uganda, for several years, but he was ready to move home to Nairobi. He had been fielding offers from several different Kenyan firms, including one of d.light's competitors.

But when Jacob saw the position at d.light and spoke to a recruiter about it in the summer of 2016, he had a strong sense that this was where he was supposed to go. "I saw the opportunity. The more I talked to the headhunter, the more excited I got," Jacob remembers. "There was this force that was pushing me to join."

Jacob was given a significant task: scale up sales and distribution of d.light's product line, especially the D30, throughout Kenya and into other African countries. Running a pilot in two counties in Kenya was one thing; making the products available to every family across the country was something else entirely. "Our biggest challenge was route to market," Jacob explains. He saw two major components to this: getting those products to customers in rural areas throughout Africa—the issue of availability—and then getting customers to take a chance on them—the issue of customer engagement.

When he joined as managing director, one of the first things Jacob did was reorganize the sales team structure in Kenya. He divided the country into five regions, with regional managers heading up each one. He subdivided those into territories, managed by territory managers, and further subdivided those into even smaller territories, led by sales executives. It was, Jacob explains, "a rationalization of distribution. We now had a footprint across the whole country. It wasn't optimal, but it was the best we could do at the time with the resources we had." By the end of 2016, d.light had team members based in every region of Kenya.

But Jacob and his team soon realized they couldn't scale up sales and distribution without a robust supporting infrastructure. The pay-go model only worked if customers actually made regular payments, and customers would only pay if they were satisfied with the product performance and after-sales service. In Kenya, the team began expanding their service center network and set up a large call center in Nairobi to handle customer registrations, questions, and complaints. But the need for after-sales services

Jacob Okoth and Ned soon after Jacob joined the company

continued to outpace what d.light could offer, forcing them to play catch-up with an increasingly impatient customer base.

The success of the Africa operations became even more crucial in late 2016, when chaos hit India. On November 8, the Indian government suddenly announced that all current 500 rupee and 1,000 rupee banknotes had been demonetized, or were no longer valid, by midnight that day. The current banknotes had to be exchanged for newly printed banknotes.[16] The demonetization caused cash shortages throughout the country, disrupting the daily lives of citizens, as well as sales for businesses across industries.

The productivity of d.light's relationships with micro-finance institutions in India had been at an all-time high, with monthly sales volumes at or exceeding 100,000 units a month. "We were at our peak in India, and then demonetization hit," Sam recalls. Without cash, customers stopped making payments and purchasing new products. Sales of the portable lanterns through micro-finance channels dropped to nearly zero. According to Sam, "We had so much inventory. This created never-ending problems for us." It would take months for d.light's India operations to begin to recover from this unexpected crisis.

The Indian government's decision to demonetize had nothing to do with d.light, but the company still bore significant consequences. That's one thing that Ned has come to understand about working in emerging markets. "Even if your business is doing well, things will happen in these markets that are outside of your control," he explains. "I've come to expect some kind of major external challenge in at least one of our core markets each year. So, we have to buffer our operations against those kinds of challenges."

With the Series D funding and expanding sales in Kenya, d.light managed to survive Indian demonetization. But the company's resources were still very finite, forcing Ned, Sam, and the rest of the leadership team to make some tough decisions. They had to slow down the speed of growth in new market entry. In countries where d.light would take the lead on sales and distribution, which were primarily in Africa, expansion into new markets could only take place one country at a time, beginning with Uganda in February 2017.

Another challenging call, which came in the middle of 2017, was the decision to end sales of the D30 and release the new X850 home

The first fleet of d.light vehicles in Kenya

system. The D30 was doing well in the market, but, at only a slightly higher price point, the X850 was a far superior product. In an ideal world, d.light would have simultaneously released a lower-cost D-series home system and the X850. But they only had enough resources to focus on one new product at a time. And they couldn't justify holding back a better product from their customers. "It was a decision to disrupt ourselves," Ned explains.

The X850 had a larger solar panel, a bigger battery, more lights, and—most exciting of all—an optional flat-screen television upgrade. Previously, d.light customers had access to lighting and mobile phone charging, and, with the D30, a radio, but a solar-powered television had always been in high demand. "We asked customers what they wanted next, and almost every customer in East Africa that we talked to wanted a TV," Ned explains. "They wanted access to information and entertainment. They felt like they were left out of the rest of the world without access to TV."

The challenge was to design a quality television that required far less power than the 20 to 400 watts used by typical televisions.[17] d.light produced a flat-screen, nineteen-inch television that used less than 10 watts of power. The design was recognized with an award from Global LEAP, an international competition of the world's best off-grid appliances.

The X850 had been under development since 2013, with the designers and engineers intentionally working at a slow pace to put the product together. "It was a more sophisticated and complex product than we had ever done before," Sam recalls.

Eva Hoffman was one of the lead designers at the time. From the very beginning, she says, "we wanted something that could eventually completely replace the grid." Their goal was to build a home system that could expand to accommodate future energy-efficient appliances such as kettles, refrigerators, and irons. "It was really fun to build something that needed to stay cheap but also was thinking about where technology would be five years later," Eva reflects.

Sam saw the development of the X850 as the culmination of all the lessons d.light had learned about customer-centric product design in the past decade. "Good design is not a democratic process," he explains. "You get design creep when a lot of other people's desires and wishes come in. But that dilutes the value of the core product for the core customers." Over four years of development, only a small number of team members participated in the design of the X850.

Introducing the X850, while removing the D30 from the market, certainly came with some risks. "There are segments in the customer pyramid that couldn't afford the X850," Jacob Okoth explains. "When we phased out the D30, we totally lost that market share." It left d.light vulnerable to competitors coming in to serve those customers.

But the decision to launch the X850 ended up paying dividends for the company. "Customers love the X850," Ned says. "That's what enabled us to create distance from our competitors."

It also helped that, by the end of 2017, the company's after-sales infrastructure was catching up to the size of their customer base in Kenya. As d.light moved into other African countries, they took the best practices from Kenya, building strong route-to-market channels and after-sales infrastructure from the outset. "As you enter new markets, you have to already start thinking about after sales and build it proportional to the expected level of growth," Jacob explains.

It's typical for businesses to wait to build a significant customer base before investing in after sales. But, according to Jacob, that doesn't work for base-of-the-pyramid customers. "You have to engage the customer from the moment they get the product. They are taking a huge risk with the product."

As all of these pieces finally began coming together—product development, marketing, sales, route to market, and after sales—no one could question d.light's leadership in the industry any longer. The company had already been the global leader in portable solar lanterns for years; by January 2018, they had become a principal provider of pay-go solar home systems as well. With the success of the X850 and the A1, they surpassed 75 million people impacted.

The goal of reaching 100 million customers by 2020—first set in 2008, just a few months after d.light had opened its offices in Shenzhen and New Delhi, and when its only product on the market was the Nova—was finally coming within reach.

Children in Vanuatu watch television for the first time with an X850 home system

Kilifi County, Kenya: Joyful Tears

Jacob Okoth and a few team members once traveled to Kilifi County in southern Kenya to deliver X850 systems to families. In one home, after they set up the system and turned on the lights, everyone—the customer's family and the d.light employees—began weeping.

"These people were just trying to make a living," Jacob remembers. The husband was a boda boda (motorbike) driver, while the wife ran a shop inside their home. Now, with the X850, she could open her shop for longer and sell more, improving their earnings and quality of life.

"It was really, really profound," Jacob explains. "I will never forget that moment."

Chapter 23

The last couple of years, according to Ned and Sam, have been really fun, in large part because of the team around them. "We have been able to attract some really talented people," Ned says. "One thing that has become more important as the company grows is to surround ourselves with the right people. And they need to be able to be empowered, in order to shine themselves."

"It's the notion that success breeds success. It gets easier as it gets bigger," adds Sam. He has been particularly impressed by the leaders that are serving d.light in management positions and on the board. "These people bring fresh, new perspectives. They've scaled companies. They are able to take this thing we've built and mold it faster."

In each area of the company, experienced and driven leaders are propelling d.light to innovate and improve on an ongoing basis. The China office continues to push for greater efficiencies and cost-effectiveness in sourcing, engineering, and manufacturing; the India office is driving new distribution models in what is still one of the toughest, most complex markets in the world; the teams in Africa, now spread across every major region of the continent, are finding more creative ways to reach their remotest customers. And in many other geographies around the world, d.light has developed a highly effective partnership model that focuses on strengthening high-integrity, indigenous distributors. This has all played a role in propelling d.light to where it is today, with the rate of expansion accelerating each year. In 2019, d.light was able to open a new office in Tanzania and significantly scale operations in Nigeria, greatly expanding their distribution reach.

Of course, all these efforts require significant manpower. From its founding team of five, to its first field offices of about ten people each, d.light today directly employs more than 1,500 people in about fifteen countries. Many of these team members are salespeople scattered across Asia, Africa, and other regions, working jobs in areas that oftentimes offer little in the way of employment opportunities.

"Some of the most exciting d.light stories that don't get told enough are the employment-generation stories," says Sam. He cites the story of Jared, who was selling used clothes at a bus depot near his home village in Kenya when he heard about d.light. He began working for a d.light solar energy promoter (SEP), doing so well

d.light now employs hundreds of customer service
representatives in call centers in Africa and India

that he himself became a SEP, and then eventually joined d.light as an official salesperson. Jared is now managing more than thirty people, while providing well for his family and making a positive impact in his community.

When the founders first started d.light, they weren't thinking about their future employees. They were focused solely on creating an affordable, high-quality light and getting it to off-grid families. But as the company has grown, so has its purpose and the kind of impact it can have. "d.light, at our core, is about more than getting people light," Ned reflects. "It's about bridging the inequality gap in the world and addressing deep social injustices. d.light has become a much bigger platform than I realized. The change has been bigger than I even imagined. We haven't just gotten people off kerosene. We've created this vehicle that has really transformed lives, both in making products and selling products. The impact has been enormous."

Another way in which Ned, Sam, and the rest of the leadership team are pursuing that impact is by entering into new product categories with their customer-centered approach. Around the time of the D30, d.light released a solar-powered fan in India. More recently, in June 2019, they partnered with American company PayJoy—founded by d.light's former head of engineering, Doug Ricket—to launch a pay-go smartphone.

"Phones are a transformative product," explains Sam. "It connects people to so many networks and platforms, and opens the door to new tools and opportunities." Phones are also strategic for helping d.light establish a loyal customer base. "When we can give customers communication, the Internet, this opens the door wide for us to cater to a much larger audience."

The launch of the smartphone in a highly competitive industry speaks to the strength of d.light's teams and partners, according to Sam. "Our quality has to be great. Our turnaround has to be great. Our customer service has to be great. Our software platforms and data analytics have to be great. The SMS providers, the telecoms, everyone has to work together. The products have to be great value for money. The sales teams have to be highly motivated. And our fundraising has to scale," he says. "All these parts have to work together in one team. Many companies do one or two of these things. It's non-trivial to do all these things together."

Nigeria: From Customer to Retailer

Valentine Okwara, the sales manager of d.light Nigeria, met a customer in eastern Nigeria who typically spent US$120 a month to purchase diesel for his generator. This provided enough electricity only for his family's most basic activities, such as cooking and getting the kids ready for school.

When the X1000 home system (a variation on the X850) became available in Nigeria, this customer quickly purchased one for a US$40 down payment and a small daily fee. The system provided enough light for the entire house for eighteen hours a day. "The cost he normally spends has been taken off him," Valentine explains.

The customer loved the X1000 so much that, within a week, he had referred ten friends from his church to d.light. From there, he decided to sign up as a d.light retailer in his local community. "We are not just taking cost away from him, we are showing him a way he can make additional money. He is most grateful," says Valentine. "He is so happy, and that makes me happy. I feel fulfilled."

Even in the midst of these successes, the learnings have continued. Some innovations, like a non-financed solar home system, fell flat right out of the gate. Finding and retaining the right people is an ongoing process. Evaluating the product needs of each market as grid electricity becomes more prevalent in places like India is a continuous challenge.

"It's not an easy thing. There's been no end of challenges," reflects Sam. "We have had to overcome them bit by bit, but often at great personal sacrifice. We've always been aligned on our North Star, the why of what we're doing, so it hasn't been hard to make those decisions. But it takes a toll." Nearly every senior leader within d.light has faced burnout or a serious health issue at some point, in large part because of the stress of managing such a complex and dynamic organization.

"Anyone who wants to do this kind of work, who wants to make this level of change, perseverance is key," Ned says. "A good degree of humility is also important. How you think it will go is not how it will happen. You have to be willing to fail, learn, adapt, and pick yourself up and do it all over again."

Despite the long odds given to d.light and its founders in the beginning, and the many mistakes and challenges along the way, that perseverance has had a sustained and growing impact. With its Series E round at the end of 2018, d.light was able to surpass US$100 million in capital raised. It took the company more than five years to reach its first 10 million customers; in 2019 alone, d.light added more than ten million customers to reach 100 million by January 2020. Much of this growth has been driven by the success of the X850, on one end of the energy access ladder, and the A2 (the next iteration of the A1) as the first step on the ladder—both of which almost weren't launched. Through the pay-go platform, d.light has essentially loaned out more than US$100 million to its customers. There are now so many people using d.light home systems that the company sometimes processes as many as ten to twenty transactions per second.

The idea of having impacted 100 million people around the globe is one that causes nearly everyone connected to the company —from the co-founders to the newest team members—to pause and consider. Co-founder Xian Wu, who married a woman he met in Hong Kong named Phoebe and now works on new technologies

A Kenyan seamstress uses the M100, the first d.light smartphone

back in his native Singapore, gets emotional when he thinks about those early days with d.light. Once, during a time of prayer, he felt led to a Bible verse that said, "Do not despise these small beginnings..."[18] Everything felt so difficult then, and every effort led to only the smallest outcome. "We planted some seeds back then, and to see what it's grown into today, there are really no words," he reflects. "It's pretty unbelievable. There are so many things that had to go right for d.light to survive against the odds and get to this stage. You can't call it anything else but a miracle."

"When I was there," remembers co-founder Gabe Risk, "we set a goal of impacting ten million people by 2015. Then that increased to twenty million, then to 100 million by 2020. It's amazing. It's incredible. And it's even more incredible that the mission of the company hasn't been lost. The focus on the customers hasn't been lost." Out of all the companies that Gabe has worked for before and since his time at d.light, "this is the one that makes me the proudest of what I did and the impact it's had."

Dave Small, the first managing director in Kenya, feels that Ned and Sam deserve particular recognition for their role in leading the company through the long, uphill climb to this point. "Those of us who came on board followed the founders' vision and their example," he says. "They are the two most modest, down-to-earth, extremely successful people that I know. Their influence was big, and they kept a lot of people going."

"One hundred million lives is not a joke," says Jacob Okoth, now the COO of d.light. "It's a huge, huge number. It's not just a business, but we're here to make an impact. There have been very many challenges along the way, and I give credit to everybody who has been part of this journey, from Ned and Sam to everyone who has played their part."

Kamal Lath agrees. "It's not just the story of Ned and Sam and the founders, but it's all the people who've been involved. It's the story of everybody. I hold this very close to myself. I don't think anything bigger will happen in my life."

The vision of d.light has also been central to convincing thousands of people—from investors and distribution partners to employees—to take a chance on a company that many didn't think would get far. It hasn't been uncommon for d.light team members to sacrifice higher paying, more stable, less demanding career opportunities to contribute to the mission of bringing light, power, and other life-changing solutions to base-of-the-pyramid families.

Kamal Lath (second from left) with d.light India partners and employees at a 2019 celebration

Former global human resources director Harry Wang was no exception, but he has no regrets. "This is something I will be proud of for my whole life. It's something you could never achieve anywhere else in the world. It can't compare with anything, with any money."

The impact of working with d.light has stayed with many former team members long after they have moved on. "Anything and everything I've ever learned today is in some part due to d.light," says Xian. Co-founder Erica Estrada-Liou has gone on to teach thousands of university students at Stanford University and the University of Maryland about human-centered design, using her experience at d.light as a primary case study.

Others have continued to stay in the social enterprise sector; still others have prioritized working for multinational firms with a strong value for people and operating with integrity. Many friendships between colleagues, forged through long days and nights with d.light, continue to this day. "It's still part of my life," says former head of marketing Tim Rump. "It wasn't a job. It was a passion."

Reaching 100 million lives impacted, however, is more than an internal goal to be celebrated. Karl Skare, now global partnerships managing director, sees this as a significant milestone for the social enterprise sector as a whole. "This is huge, and I think we haven't

Employees in the China office celebrate the company's tenth anniversary

even really thought through how important this is. It's not just 100 million lives, but also achieving financial success. We recently surpassed 100 million dollars in annual revenue and have been sustainably profitable for several years. This is a case study, a proof point for the viability of social enterprise."

But the heart of d.light remains, to this day, the families with no or unreliable electricity that inspired the venture to begin with. Sam still keeps in touch with the boy, now a young man, who was burned in that kerosene fire so many years ago in Benin. He called Sam up to personally thank him when Sam sent him a Nova.

In a recent visit to Cote D'Ivoire with a distribution partner, Sam found himself in a village that was remarkably similar to the village in Benin where he had lived for four years as a Peace Corps volunteer. It was stiflingly hot. There were mud huts everywhere. They had to gain approval from the village elder before talking with families there. Someone killed a chicken to serve to Sam and the other guests.

"But the difference," says Sam, "is they've got a solar panel on their roof. They've got a TV on the table. They're connected to the world. One day they're using kerosene, and the next day they've got all these lights, a radio, and a TV, all for a small down payment. If you think about the situation, it's insane."

A customer he encountered in Kenya explained it this way: "I've got my TV, and the rich people have their TV. The rich people might have a forty-inch TV, and mine is twenty-four inches. But we're watching the same thing."

"It's a massive levelizer," Sam reflects.

The two co-founders are happy to celebrate this 100 million lives milestone, but they are already looking ahead, thinking about the next stage for d.light. "It's definitely satisfying to accomplish this huge goal, and on time," says Ned. "But I feel a sense of restlessness also, because we've built this platform now that has potential to do so much more. There's a sense of not wanting to celebrate too long. We have a lot more to do. Our work isn't done."

Sam agrees. "It's like we're summiting Everest, but we're just at base camp," he says. "But we are getting there, and that's what's motivating."

Afterword
A New Vision for a New Decade

BY NED TOZUN AND SAM GOLDMAN

d.light may have started small, but we always dreamed big. From the beginning, we were driven by a belief that people living without reliable electricity around the world deserved a brighter, more equitable future. We were convinced that this could be addressed through clean energy solutions that were sustainable for families and for the planet.

Along the way, we decided to set the bold goal of enabling 100 million people to get off kerosene by 2020. We had little idea of how we would get there. But we knew we would have to pick the mountain we wanted to climb if we had any chance of reaching a higher elevation.

The journey has been more challenging and complex than we ever anticipated. We shifted from a solar lantern company to a solar energy company; from a product company to a product, distribution, and financing company. And, along the way, we've managed to create that most elusive of entities: a truly triple-bottom-line business. It gives us great pride to know that as our operations grow, social impact and positive environmental impact increase as well.

Though there are certainly things we would have done differently, we are immensely proud of what d.light has been able to achieve. In addition to actually meeting that 100-million-people-impacted goal, we have helped build a robust off-grid energy industry. We've directly and indirectly provided jobs for tens of thousands of people, many of them living in regions where stable employment is sorely lacking.

As we look ahead to the future, we are still driven by many of the same values that we debated alongside our co-founders, Xian, Gabe, and Erica, in the classrooms and outdoor spaces of Stanford University. We are still inspired by the same vision that has, over the past thirteen years, compelled many talented, passionate people—both young and more experienced—to invest in d.light through their skills, ideas, energy, and resources.

Our strategic approach to the future work of d.light is built upon these beliefs:

1. We believe in a world with equality for all people.

2. We believe in making life brighter now and in the future.

3. We believe in solutions that fight climate change and are good for the planet.

4. We believe the powerful forces of capitalism, technology, and human creativity can be harnessed and directed in a way to make this change happen more quickly and at a larger scale than previously imagined.

5. We believe we already have the people, technology, and solutions necessary to create the change we want to see.

Having had the privilege to learn from villagers, entrepreneurs in emerging markets, business leaders, public sector officials, and academics, we believe income inequality and climate change are two of the greatest challenges humanity is currently facing. And we believe d.light has a role to play in addressing these challenges.

The longer we have been leading d.light, the greater the potential we see for this organization to create positive social change. We want to expand our vision to meet that potential and set our sights on the next, even greater mountain to scale.

MISSION: As of 2020, we are expanding our mission beyond energy. **Our new mission is to transform lives with sustainable products.**

BRAND PROMISE: Because we want our products to have positive social and environmental impacts right away and for the long term, we will be guided by **a new brand promise: making life brighter.**

VALUES: The i.HOPE values that have steered us — Innovation, Honesty, Optimism, Passion, and Empathy —will continue to serve as our guiding light in our decision-making, our culture, our partnerships, and our role in society.

GOAL: We believe that the scope of the problems we face as a planet require bold initiatives that create scalable and lasting change. Therefore, we are setting our sights on having an even greater impact: **Our goal is to transform 1 billion lives with sustainable products by 2030.**

Living out this vision will require the best of our energy and the best of who we are. But with the ongoing support of d.light's amazing employees, board members, customers, partners, and investors, we believe this is possible.

As we have seen throughout d.light's history, positive change can happen. And if all of humanity is to thrive, it *must* happen. We are both humbled and honored by the opportunity to contribute to this change.

Let's make life brighter together, now and for generations to come.

Acknowledgements

Every day, we are aware that d.light would not be where it is except for the incredible support we have received from thousands of individuals along the way. Most of these people provided assistance for no reason except their desire to see us successfully bring solar energy to off-grid families. Many sacrificed time and other valuable resources without asking for anything in return.

To all of you who offered advice, connected us, provided encouragement, gave money, volunteered, shared the word—thank you. We are grateful for the many kind and generous souls that exist in this world.

While it would not be possible to name everyone who has contributed to the d.light journey, we'd like to recognize a few who went above and beyond to support us.

First, we are grateful to Xian, Gabe, and Erica, for being incredible partners and friends from day one until today. You each played a pivotal role in planting seeds of ingenuity, integrity, and empathy into the DNA of d.light that will forever be there.

It's impossible to overstate the role that the Stanford d.school and GSB played in inspiring us, equipping us, and providing key resources to get us started. Thank you in particular to Jim Patell, George Kembel, and David Kelley for your guidance and encouragement, especially when we were still clueless students. And thank you to Jim and Debbie Taylor from Proximity Designs, who taught us so many in-the-field lessons about design, sales, and distribution in emerging markets—and also kindly hosted us in their home several times.

To our first employees in India, China, Tanzania, and Kenya: thanks for being willing to take a chance on us, even when it required great personal sacrifice. Thank you to John Schram, Michael Marks, Michael Dearing, and Tom Bird, who provided invaluable advice in the critical early stages and were among our first angel investors. Thanks also to our first large-scale investors, including Acumen, Garage, Draper Fisher Jurvetson, Gray Matters Capital, Nexus India Capital, and Mahindra, for taking the risk to give us capital without any guarantees of a return.

Jacqueline Novogratz, you are a force to be reckoned with. Your patient capital and your influence have saved d.light many times. We are so grateful for your willingness to give all of yourself toward social change. Thank you also for writing such a heartfelt foreword for this book.

Stuart Davidson, thank you for being a foundational adviser, partner, and friend when you were board chair during d.light's darkest days. Your unwavering support and trust in us made all the difference.

When it comes to team members, we count ourselves among the luckiest in the world. Thank you to our d.light employees and their families around the world, who give so much of themselves to our mission each and every day.

To our families: Thank you for tolerating our long hours and even longer business trips. Thank you for creating home wherever in the world we asked you to go. We could not have done any of this without your love and support.

And, finally, to the 100 million and more d.light customers worldwide: Thank you for continuing to inspire us, to challenge us, to hold us accountable, to push us to do the best we can. We are honored to be a part of your lives.

— NED AND SAM

I would never have been part of the d.light story except that I fell in love with a wide-eyed entrepreneur who wanted nothing less than to change the world. Thank you, Ned, for giving me the opportunity to walk alongside you on this incredible road, to grow my faith and courage, and to meet so many exceptional people along the way.

I'm grateful to Sam and Ned for entrusting me with the d.light story, and giving me the chance to both hear and record the extraordinary experiences of the last fifteen years. Thank you to the more than twenty d.light employees, past and present, who generously shared with me their greatest triumphs and disappointments during their time with the company.

Many thanks to my mother and mother-in-law, who gave countless hours toward entertaining and loving on our two high-energy boys, thus giving me the time to write this book.

And a special thanks to Boyani Omwenga, who powered through many late nights to help make this book happen.

To all the hardworking team members at d.light: You are my heroes. Keep reaching for that brighter future.

— DORCAS

Endnotes

1. "Internal Conflict in Peru," *Wikipedia*. accessed December 16, 2019, en.wikipedia.org/wiki/Internal_conflict_in_Peru.

2. Sanni, Ahmed, Oduwole, Ebunoluwa, O.o, Odusanya, & A., Fadeyibi. (2003). "Contaminated Kerosene Burn Disasters in Lagos, Nigeria." *Annals of Burns and Fire Disasters*, Volume XVI, 208-212.

3. International Finance Corporation, "LEDs for Developing Countries: A $40 billion market" (seminar, October 16, 2006).

4. Aspen Institute Initiative for Social Innovation through Business and World Resources Institute, "Beyond Grey Pinstripes 2003: Preparing MBAs for Social and Environmental Stewardship," assets.aspeninstitute.org/content/uploads/files/content/upload/bgps_2003_brochure.pdf.

5. "Northern Cyprus," *Wikipedia*, accessed February 13, 2020, en.wikipedia.org/wiki/Northern_Cyprus.

6. Asian Development Bank, *Myanmar: Status and Potential for the Development of Biofuels and Rural Renewable Energy*, 2009.

7. "Sun Microsystems," *Wikipedia*, accessed December 16, 2019, en.wikipedia.org/wiki/Sun_Microsystems.

8. d.light business plan for the Global Social Venture Competition, April 2007, 12.

9. Shepard, Wade, "A Look Inside Shenzhen's High-Tech Empire," *Forbes*, July 14, 2016, forbes.com/sites/wadeshepard/2016/07/14/a-look-inside-shenzhens-high-tech-empire/#666057bd4f36.

10. International Finance Corporation, "Lighting Asia: Solar Off-Grid Lighting: Market Analysis of India, Bangladesh, Nepal, Pakistan, Indonesia, Cambodia and Philippines," February 2012, scribd.com/document/94562235/Lighting-Asia-Solar-Off-Grid-Lighting-Market-Analysis-of-India-Bangladesh-Nepal-Pakistan-Indonesia-Cambodia-and-Philippines.

11. Amadeo, Kimberly, "2008 Financial Crisis Timeline: Critical Events in the Worst Crisis Since the Depression," *The Balance*, updated November 20, 2019, thebalance.com/2008-financial-crisis-timeline-3305540.

12. Bajaj, Vikas, "Microlender, First in India to Go Public, Trades Higher," *New York Times*, August 16, 2010, nytimes.com/2010/08/17/business/global/17micro.html.

13. International Institute for Sustainable Development and Global Subsidies Initiative, "Kerosene Subsidies in India: The status quo, challenges and the emerging path to reform" May 2017, .iisd.org/sites/default/files/publications/kerosene-in-india-staus-quo-path-to-reform.pdf.

14. Rai, Mineet, "India's Microfinance Crisis is a Battle to Monopolize the Poor," *Harvard Business Review*, November 4, 2010, hbr.org/2010/11/indias-microfinance-crisis-is.

15. "M-Pesa," *Wikipedia*, accessed December 16, 2019, en.wikipedia.org/wiki/M-Pesa.

16. "Indian Banknote Demonetisation," *Wikipedia*, accessed December 16, 2019, en.wikipedia.org/wiki/2016_Indian_banknote_demonetisation.

17. Austin, Ryan, "How Many Watts Does a TV Use? You Might Be Surprised," *Understand Solar*, July 2, 2017, understandsolar.com/how-many-watts-does-a-tv-use.

18. Zechariah 4:10 (New Living Translation).

Made in the USA
Las Vegas, NV
15 April 2021